JOURNEYING WITH GOD

D0300017

Journeying with God

PARADIGMS OF POWER AND POWERLESSNESS

Austin Smith

Sheed & Ward
London

Nihil obstat Anton Cowan, Censor
Imprimatur † John Crowley, V.G., Bishop in Central London, Westminster,
26 June 1990

ISBN 0 7220 4660 X

Copyright © 1990 by Austin Smith

First published in 1990 by Sheed & Ward Ltd
2 Creechurch Lane, London EC3A 5AQ
Filmset by Fakenham Photosetting Ltd, Fakenham
Printed and bound in Great Britain
by BPCC Wheatons Ltd, Exeter

All rights reserved. No part of this book may be reproduced, stored in a
retrieval system, or transmitted, in any form, or by any means, electronic,
mechanical, photocopying, recording or otherwise, without permission in
writing from the publishers

Book production by Bill Ireson

Contents

Contents

Preface

This book is the consequence of innumerable conversations. It is a meditation upon those conversations. And it is a meditation upon my life as a religious and a priest. If it helped to foster further conversations I would be pleased. The conversations have not been ungrounded in action. Quite the contrary. And I would never have attempted to write it were it not for the requests by many, who have been part of the conversations and the action of life, to do so. Therefore I thank all those friends and co-workers for their encouragement.

I would like to thank specifically Nicholas Postlethwaite, Joseph Ward, Michael Bold and John Sherrington, my fellow Passionists in Inner City life and action, who have been part of the daily conversation; Mary McAleese and Julia Battye for their encouragement.

Finally, by way of gratitude, I must mention John Fitzsimons, John Orme Mills, O.P., and Bill Glen-Doepel, for their help, suggestions, criticisms and editorial work.

Austin Smith, C.P.

CHAPTER ONE

Matters Personal and Impersonal

It is a highly dangerous enterprise to declare oneself, to offer one's spiritual self, publicly for scrutiny. Yet, as Iris Murdoch once put it talking about Sartre:

> A philosophy cannot be a total system because the world is contingent and infinitely various, and systematic philosophy is often made more readable as well as more reasonable by the personal interests of the philosopher, by the way in which his analyses and examples stray toward particular matters which have amazed him or frightened him or pleased him; so that his book may have turned out to be more personal and accidental than he intended.[1]

But if one pursues that path or finds oneself forced onto that path, no matter how much objective analysis one wishes to communicate, the outcome is finally personal and the critique is personal.

I would like to write or sketch out a "systematic liberation theology" for the United Kingdom. I cannot do it. And, to be absolutely honest, I am not sure that I should even attempt it. I say this not simply because I am unsure of my own capability of doing so, but because I have a feeling that Christianity in the United Kingdom has not yet sufficiently declared its own insecurity; it has not asked a sufficient number of questions about itself. I don't believe that any institution is able to respond to critical voices from outside until it has been able to question its own voice. The problem is that it will never do the latter until it has done the former.

If there is a declaration of insecurity in the Church, it is of an abstract nature. Though it may admit failure, too many discussions are conducted in terms of large concepts: the materialism of the times, failure of the family, failure of the educational system, etc. Such an approach distracts from any radical analysis of the inner causes of insecurity. Like so many of us who as individuals feel or know our own insecurity, we run away from it by blaming others or by retreating into generalised analyses of the world.

I also believe that any liberation theology for the United Kingdom will need to take into account a whole area of political, social, economic and cultural history which is quite distinctive in the context of "freedom". For example, Welfare is an historical phenomenon in our history. It goes as far back as the Tudor Poor Law reforms of 1536–1601 and even in the pre-First World War era there were innovations.

Welfare can so easily distract us from authentic definitions of poverty. A liberation theology would need to take account of trade unionism in both its origins and evolution. And, specifically at a theological level, the relationship between Church and State in the United Kingdom would call for in-depth examination. No liberation theology can be developed in the United Kingdom today without a profound sensitivity to the question of racism, as an evil, and multi-culturalism as a liberating power for good. Finally, unlike in other contexts of liberation theology the disjunction between the sacred and the secular, a distinction with which, admittedly, some of us feel uneasy is nevertheless very pronounced. These are just some of the points I think would need to be considered in any attempt to formulate such a liberation theology. On the positive side, however, there is much Christian social thought and action to be drawn upon.

The mutual exchange, with its concern and awareness has begun, but it is early days. One only hopes that it will be encouraged by "official ministering Christianity". "Inner-cityism" is a cancer developing in the body politic. Whatever the encouragement should be or wherever it may come from, this much is certain: those who have experienced or been part of this political, social, economic and cultural illness must bear witness to it and must create the context for those who suffer from its relentless growth to speak. I am the last to believe that you can reduce Christianity, the Church, the priesthood, the religious life, indeed society itself, to individual personal responses and interpretations. At the same time, the major debates about Christianity and society are fed by personal responses, personal attitudes and personal philosophies and theologies.

In this book, then, I offer a personal witness and reflection, set against a larger backdrop and from within the midst of my own personal life journey as a priest and a religious.

I was born in the City of Liverpool and returned to it, to one part of its inner city, in 1970. The return and the area to which I returned raised different questions than the ones of my Catholic upbringing and education. At the same time the seeds of later questions had been sown in my childhood, for even then the social and the political reality were very firmly brought home to me, especially by my father. This took place on two levels. I knew very early on about his trade union activity; and I knew, too, the near despair of unemployment. I lived in a home which for many years had to "make do". A visit from the Unemployment Assistance Board meant shovels of coal being hastily taken off the fire and fresh milk removed from the table. Even having a piano could affect what you got from the UAB man.

There was also an extraordinary respect for schoolteachers in my home when I was a child, expressed chiefly by my mother. I am not quite sure what teachers symbolised: a safety of job or depth of wisdom. Probably the former; but if the teacher was also a nun, then earthly security was combined with a certain heavenly security. Anyway this much I know, even if my parents did not know it: they, my parents, ultimately gave me a greater sense of both heavenly and earthly security than teachers or teaching nuns ever offered. Later years of retreats and conferences have confirmed my suspicions on both fronts.

This is not some expression of class-consciousness, but

rather an attempt to say that the growth of professionalism, not by any means to be ignored or trivialised, so easily ends up oppressing ordinary people's own self-confidence. This applies in matters both secular and sacred, to use again that somewhat suspect distinction. If my life, as priest and religious, in the Inner City has done anything to me personally, it has above all things led me to a profound respect for and wonder at the depth of power in the lives of the powerless.

I take a walk from time to time these days around the refurbished docklands of Liverpool. As I do so, I find myself embraced by both a past and a present. The River Mersey is part of my life. My grandparents sailed up it in search of a new life. They were a few amongst thousands who made the same journey, while thousands sailed down the Mersey to other lands. It is a river which has known great sorrow and great joy; it is a symbol of a journey into freedom for some and into oppression for others. Whatever technical definition we wish to give to the Inner City, the underlying experience (i.e. powerlessness) is not to be understood simply in terms of the sociological research of the 1950s and 1960s. The Inner City is, rather, the expression of an invariable historical truth, namely that the powerless of this world do not create themselves – they are the inevitable product of the powerful.

Thus, when I reflect upon and, where and when possible, act with my black friends in this city, I know I am not only existing and acting with a present experience, but also with "a history". I have thought during my dockside walk about the sixty vessels annually, on an average, which "between 1748 and 1784 cleared Liverpool for Africa for slaves"[2]. Those voyages were part of Liverpool's creation of wealth. It has been suggested that Liverpool during those years invested £264,000 in the slave trade annually. "Up to 1807, between 40 and 100 slave ships visited Africa annually."[3] And I have often recalled the words of this document:

LADING BILL OF A CARGO OF SLAVES

Shipped by the grace of God and in good order, and well conditioned, by James Dodd (of the City of Liverpool), in and upon the good ship *Thomas* (of the Port of Liverpool), master of this present voyage, under God, Captain Peter Roberts (of the City of Liverpool), and now at anchor at Calabar, and by God's grace bound for Jamaica, with 630 slaves, men and women, branded DD, and numbered in the margin 31 DD, and are to be delivered in good order, and well conditioned, at the Port of Kingston (the dangers of the seas and mortality only excepted), unto Messrs Broughton and Smith. In witness whereof the master and the purser of the ship *Thomas* hath affirmed this bill of lading, and God speed the Good ship to her destined Port in safety.

AMEN. October 21 1767[4]

Each man and woman had the space of a coffin to lie down. With such a history and in the midst of a contemporary crippling racism my friends live with love and hope today. But the question is not about my liberating them. I cannot do that unless I am open to liberation by them. If there is to be such a thing as a liberation theology in my own world, I believe now that the issue of racism and the struggle with racism, both personally and institutionally, must be an essential aspect of its construction. Attempting to struggle with it and understand it has been one of the most crucial experiences of my own life in the Inner City.

When I first came to it, I believe I came intent, so to speak, upon a work or an apostolate. I did not expect – perhaps did not want – the experience to demand personal change in the priorities of my belief in and understanding of God. I did not expect – again, perhaps did not want – to be led into a reflection upon Church and priesthood, which would lead not only to a questioning about how the Church should be and act in the Inner City, but how the Church should be and act in society at large. On the one hand, I see the need for a new philosophical and theological journey; but, on the other, I find myself able to offer only a personal witness. There are and there will be other witnesses. The important thing is that such witnessing should give rise to a liberating conversation, in the name of the liberation of us all. Without such a conversation major documents on the Inner City, no matter how inspiring and educative they may be, remain without roots. So I invite you to meditate with me about the phenomenon of powerlessness in our time, of marginalisation and stigmatisation, concretely experienced in the Inner City, which poses questions not only about Christianity, the Church and the Inner City, but also about Christianity and the Church in our time.

In one of their many recorded conversations, Sartre says to Simone du Beauvoir:

> You and I, for example, have lived without paying attention to the problem, I don't think many of our conversations have been concerned with it . . . And yet we've lived; we feel that we've taken an interest in our world and we've tried to understand it.[5]

The "problem" Sartre refers to is God. I could never say that. There is a sense in which God has totally dominated my life, both as a problem and a solution. Indeed, God has been at the heart of both my interest in, and understanding of, the world. How this central presence of God in my life may have adverse effects upon others or distorts my understanding of the world or causes a certain exclusivity in my thought and action, are other questions entirely. None of us can act as reliable judge of our own cause. Therefore the final judgement made or sentence passed must be left to others.

But I need to qualify a distinction already made. God as a problem and God as a solution have in my life been wrapped up in each other. There have been times when God the solution has been a problem and when God the problem has been a solution. For example, God invoked as a solution in helping us all on our materialistic and competitive journeying through life has been a problem. The problem God of the crucified Jesus has been, and remains, a solution.

I need, too, to qualify the statement, "God has totally dominated my life." Domination is an ill-chosen word – there is a ring of oppression about it. Better for me to say that, from my earliest years, God has been part of my life. God was given to me at birth, I might almost say, was simultaneous with my conception. Regularly invoked in my home and an essential part of my schooling, I could not escape God's presence. I have to admit, especially in my early schooling, there was a sense when he did begin to be, if I may so put it, somewhat fascist in his projected action and image. He was used to frighten me.

And he's turned up that way from time to time in life. In my childhood, however, he was very gentle indeed. In fact he was so gentle that Christian pulpit thunderings, not to mention some rather stupid Catholic educational efforts at frightening me in his name, made very little lasting impact. I suppose it is true to say that God was equated with authority, and my first taste of authority, namely my parents, was very firm, yet very gentle. Thus, they gave God a rather good name. I would not want to impose later sophistications upon early simplicities; it is always a danger. At the same time, I would want to say that God was made comfortably part of being human. God was part of the total scene. God was male and female, in the very best sense of the words, though historically my parents were of their times, times which insisted upon the "He/Him" of God. When my parents said, as they did very often, that God had been good to them, they had been very good for God as far as I was concerned.

In spite of the very difficult era in which I was brought up, I was always given the impression that nobody need despair. And the basic reason for this on-going hopefulness rested in God. Of course, people did despair; people died well before their time; people were crushed by the oppressions of the day; and my father fought so many things on the political front. I make this point, however, not to justify a naive apologetic for God's existence, but to attempt to communicate the fact that I was brought up to see God, not in some vast judgemental way, but reaching deep into the ordinary world of a human being's hopes and despairs. And this God was given to me on the side of the powerless or, to use that rather charming biblical expression, on the side of the "little ones". To be sure, my parents were children of their own age, in the sense that they shared in a certain spirituality of resignation. But since there was a good deal of political and economic critique in my home, the acceptance of such a spirituality was subjected both to qualification and careful scrutiny. For example, my father would have found somewhat hard to take, to put it mildly, the words in a sermon of a Flemish bishop in the early years of the nineteenth century:

> Divine providence has preordained that some of us be poor, and some of us be rich. This is one of the most evident proofs of God's goodness and wisdom. Indeed, the inequality is the most solid bond that ties classes together. To a certain extent it may seem that God abandons those who are crushed under the burden of misery. However, from a wider perspective, he "employs" their poverty to recommend them to the charity of the rich.[6]

For the most part I do believe that all of us who have a belief in God relativise him. I have known ambitious parents more theistically rebellious about the existence of an all-caring deity in the face of their daughter's A-levels failure than with the tragedies of Ethiopian famine. The naked God, if I may put it so, is politically, socially, economically and culturally, up for grabs. And certainly for many the God of Golgotha is alright when associated with reminders about a failure in charity, but not too acceptable when he may be asking some questions about changing social and political structures.

It was not "just God" who dominated my life. The God I was given, the God I have accepted at the centre of my life, has been, and is, for better or worse, somewhat fiercely institutionalised, and there is no doubt in my own mind that such institutionalisation has brought many confusions. If God in himself did not mentally colonise my parents' minds, but rather opened up to them a vision of freedom, the institutional God certainly involved a tendency towards spiritual and mental colonisation. Once one enters – or for that matter is born into – a formal and institutional religion, the image of God becomes, in a very special way, kaleidoscopic.

I don't see many kaleidoscopes around these days but I remember them well as a child. You looked through the tube at a pattern of colours. Then you shook the tube, looked again, and got a new pattern. Now I know this can happen with images of God without the institution; you can get a sequence of different images of God. The quest of the philosophers and the mystics has been rich in this regard; but if one takes formal religion, for example, Roman Catholicism, as the kaleidoscope, every shake of the institution produces a different pattern of God. Thus the image of God comes to depend upon who shakes the kaleidoscope and – which is a much more subtle historical question – when and where it is shaken. It is all very well to say there is a reality called magisterial teaching or an authoritative teaching voice, but one can't get away from the kaleidoscopic reality as viewed by various human beings. Remember the already quoted Flemish bishop! What I am attempting to say, as gently as possible, is that though God may be considered the overall power, one can't escape the fact that God is not without masters and mistresses. When it comes to "teaching about God", the frontier between interpretation and manipulation is very faintly drawn upon the theological map. To put it another way, in formalised religion God is highly dependent for his good name – not to say his bad name – upon those who have taken, been elected or appointed to or born into, the power points of the institution.

When I was a youngster (things they say have changed radically now, but we'll need to come to that eventually), God had a Church building on a particular plot of land, it was the centre of the parish and Fr Smith ran the whole project on God's behalf. In strict reflective, theological and spiritual terms nobody thought Fr Smith was God. But God in practical terms, not to say theoretical terms, got his respect, position and status through Fr Smith. And whilst, on the basis of sheer ordinary instinct face to face with authority, the "ordinary" faithful knew where to draw the line and distinguish between God and Smith, confusions were not unknown. God all too often got a very bad name because of Smith; Smith too often got an unmerited good name because of God. And, of course, God found glory, wonder and profound love because of the dedication, service and commitment of so many priests in his ministry. The Gospel has a habit, as Gilson once said of philosophy, of burying its own undertakers. For this reason a compelling and awe-inspiring image of God has so often, throughout history, broken through.

I would be the last to quarrel with Heidegger's distinction between unconditional character of faith and the questioning quality of human thought as radically distinct worlds. The only problem is the distinction becomes somewhat confusing, to say the least, when we promote a religion in which God is revealed – indeed speaks – through the human. Indeed it becomes highly confusing when I am asked to contemplate a God screaming for water on a Friday afternoon. Yes, I do believe in God but I wish to struggle with a God, or at least the meaning of a God, who has become part of human history. To put this another way, struggling with the impact of a priest-hood, of a Church, agreeing to mediate the meaning of God through human beings, dependent upon human beings, seems to me wrapped up in my believing in God. One can't opt out of humanity at that point, where human action or human experi-ence becomes somewhat puzzling when faced with God's existence and action. In other words, the power of God becomes highly exposed to questioning when it surrenders its interpretation, not to say its communication, to the ambiva-lences and ambiguities of human power. In such a situation we cannot remove the power of God from human questioning. We cannot do so because it is in the process of being mediated by humanity, and any human mediation implies an exercise of human power. It seems to me that far too many games are played – more often than not games with complicated and tortuous rules – with the counters of divine and human power and their interdependence. Some would say it has always been so. If that is the case all the more reason for on-going vigilance.

Such a question seems to be more and more central to my thought and action, not to mention prayer, in the Inner City. The years in an Inner City ministry, twelve of which I also spent as a prison chaplain, have increasingly led me beyond the boundaries of an Inner City and prison chaplaincy. They are years which have raised questions not simply about God and institutional Church vis-à-vis the Inner City, but about God and the institutional Church itself.

There is something about existing and acting with the pow-erless of this world which leads one beyond the fact and experience of powerlessness. A question constantly surfacing in my mind, as I pursue my life and ministry, concerns who defines and how do we define the process of life? If, as I have already admitted in this meditation, God has been at the very centre of my life, such a question leads me to ask: "Who is God, and how is he to be defined?" In other words if many of us see God in the driving seat in life's journeying, no matter how we define such an activity in God, then it would seem to be vitally important that we find out how we are defining or describing God. The process of questioning is such not only because God is central to my understanding of life, but also because God is invoked by so many who draw up an agenda for living which leads too often to the creation or perpetuation of the powerless.

I feel I have lived through a decade of high political insensitivity face to face with the powerless of our own society. The insensitivity is seldom really debated. I understand this in political life because politicians must come to grips with, as indeed we all must, the concrete measures which lead to marginalisation and oppression. But one cannot help wondering about the dignity and nobility of political life when a vote for a party is seen as a major criterion of the rightness and wrongness of the measures under discussion. I have heard politicians making such remarks as: "Well, we were warned not to do this or that, but we did it and not only found favour, our vote increased." That is a form of pragmatism and utilitarianism which leads to ultimate social and spiritual suicide. Indeed, it is a mode of judging the moral and ethical content of life by way of mathematical criteria. If those who so think also claim the need for and necessity of God at the centre of our lives, then we are faced with a potentially degrading definition of God. Quality of life and action is tyrannised by a quantitative factor.

I have made a distinction between the reality and personality of God in all its nakedness and the God who has become part of my life by way of mediations. One mediation has been my home background. But another mediation, closely interwoven with my home background, has been institutional religion. In such a paradigm the power of God has come through human power. One may validly say that God has been *in that human power*. While considering the danger of seeing God identified with that human power, I must scrutinise that human power in order to satisfy myself that it truly is a mediation of God. In the last analysis I am suggesting that such an examination is wrapped up in my act of belief in God. In other words, those who define life in the light of their understanding of God must be closely questioned about their definition of life. At the end of the day I am suggesting that definitions of God can never be neutral; they are always subject to vested interests. This is crucial when faced with an historical religion which considers itself a "teacher of and about God". One must never blindly believe in any mediation of God, no matter how exalted it may be, without subjecting it to continual scrutiny. This is a *sine qua non* of human and Christian maturing and maturity.

I would like to invite you to share a personal exercise, directed towards the examination and understanding of the mediations which rule our lives. I will call it "The Clock of Influence".

CHAPTER TWO

The Clock of Influence

It was early autumn. I remember there were flowers growing. It was over forty years ago. In those days the stationmaster grew flowers to brighten up the junction platform. I have been at the same junction since; there are no flowers now. There are, however, a great deal of graffiti. But when I set out on my journey, waiting for the train to take me on my journey to "become a priest" the walls were clean. It is vital, nevertheless, to point out that the absence of graffiti should not be perceived as an indication that there was nothing to protest against, nobody to love or detest. In fact there were some rather frightened efforts of pen-knife engravers. The comparative cleanliness should be attributed, I would think, more to the absence in those days of aerosol sprays and felt-pens than to the lack of desire, in various sectors of the public, to address their fellow citizens about their bitterness or enchantment with life.

In fact there was a lot to be bitter about in that early autumn forty years ago. We had just come to the end of one of a series of global killings. The time had come to number such killings, and the one just finished would be known for the future as the Second World War. It had come to an end with an act which had not really sunk into our consciousness. Two atomic bombs had been dropped on Japan. In Hiroshima, in the words of an eye-witness, "the bomb exploded in one instant, 260,000 people died and many more were injured. And people continue to die and die because of that one atom bomb." The world would never be the same again. To use the chilling poetic language of our own time, we were *now* in an era of a possible nuclear winter. Possibility was all that was needed to create a new world. One did not need an actual nuclear winter to change our global view of human existence; a possible one would do. Personal contingency had come to be overshadowed by possible global annihilation. It is hard to believe, yet it is true, but I was to go through over seven years of formation and never once, in any analytical way – apart from some vague discussions about the morality of the "just war" – was this event referred to.

The United Kingdom, then, had just begun to create its Welfare State. There seemed to be a vision not so much of false greatness, but a vision of nobody being in need. The poor were going to face a different future. People spoke also about old oppressions passing away, colonialism was believed to be breathing its last. These topics, however, did not seem to occupy us very much in our formative years towards priesthood. I heard a great deal about the Education Act and the fight for Catholic schools, but not a great deal was heard about this new world we thought, or believed, was coming to birth.

Anyway, there I was on the junction platform "going away", to use the terminology of Catholic culture, "to become a priest". Apart from my parents there were some people from the parish on the same platform. They said to my parents that "they should be very proud". I am sure they did not believe they were defining priesthood, but they certainly had their view of it: it was irrevocable – and it was not a very good thing to "come home" once you'd gone. I was being put into a position of living up to Catholic cultural expectations. Of course, I had to live up to ideals and commitments in the name of God, but all cultures to a certain extent are created by social relationships, and the Catholic cultural view of the priesthood was no exception.

There was another friend on the platform that day. He was a Jewish friend of the family. He also said to my parents that they "should be very proud". He had been informed about millions of his brothers and sisters dying by gas, the bullet, the rope or starvation. One would think, with Adorno: "After Auschwitz there is no word tinged from on high, not even a theological one, that has any right unless it underwent transformation.''[1] Yet "The Holocaust" was to play very little part in my formation. Perhaps it was a question of time. Maybe each of us was asking ourself the question Steiner put to himself and – like him – answering ourself: "What is there to *say* about Belsen? Nothing."[2]

Don't misunderstand me – I was very happy on that early autumn day amidst the stationmaster's wallflowers. It was adventure, it was wonder, it was not just a physical railway junction, it was a major junction in my life. And now years later I have no regrets. In my own naive and immature way at that point in life I saw myself called by God. I still believe I am called by God. The call from God is to be located in the mediations of life. If I were to illustrate the mediations generically which, so to speak, made up God, I would offer the following "Clock of Influence" as I have called it:

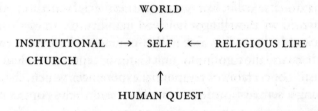

$$\text{WORLD}$$
$$\downarrow$$
$$\text{INSTITUTIONAL} \quad \rightarrow \quad \text{SELF} \quad \leftarrow \quad \text{RELIGIOUS LIFE}$$
$$\text{CHURCH}$$
$$\uparrow$$
$$\text{HUMAN QUEST}$$

The point I am making is that the power of God is concretised for me in the concretisation of the life-points of my "Clock of Influence". Thus there is a sense in which God is the world, God is the institutional Church, God is the religious life and God is the human quest. I write metaphorically. I am not identifying the nature of God with the chosen points of influence, but I am saying it is only through such points that I find the power of God, indeed the meaning of God, mediated to me. And they are mediated to me in very concrete ways.

For forty years certainly those points in my life have remained, but the concretisation of those mediations has radically altered. Indeed, the very relationship between the four mediations, in terms of priority, importance, richness and starting points, in all my thought, action and prayer, has also undergone very radical change.

God's mediations are grasped by time – I would prefer to say, are embraced by time. For example, Bernard of Clairvaux in the twelfth century knew and experienced World, Institutional Church, Human Quest and Religious Life. He may well have so eternalised *his* understanding of these points of influence where his particular mediations of God were found to leave me with a problem. In other words, he may well have suggested to his world, and my world, that his understanding of God's mediation was without change. In other words, God became a twelfth-century citizen somewhat unwilling, if not unable, to live in any other century with a comfortable authenticity. The "Clock of Clairvaux", in other words, is simply not mine, no matter how instructive it may be about the eternal movements and words of God.

I have to say that I feel myself to be part of an institutional Church, and more specifically in a priesthood, which is in the depths of its collective consciousness frightened of this, because of an unwillingness or an inability to accept a new "Clock of Influence" which will offer new mediations of God. This fear will not go away unless we accept the "relentless criticism" of certain contemporary experiences which, though arousing a sense of profound anxiety, nevertheless opens new doors.

I would not presume to pass judgement upon the rightness or wrongness of his mediations, but rather ask what was the meaning of such an interpretation of God for a man of the twelfth century. But having understood this, it is crucial that his interpretation is not allowed to imprison my search for meaning. Just as your and my understanding of God's mediation must not bind a twenty-first-century man or woman, so the mediations of a twelfth-century man or woman, or indeed an early twentieth-century man or woman, must not be allowed to imprison us. Our failure to analyse and understand historical meaningfulness is the root cause of so much "dialogue of the deaf". For me, living community is simply "conversation".

Within our lives, the changes in the "Clock of Life" may well be no more than a matter of our own personal evolution, but they can also originate in a wider historical crisis. It has been suggested that:

> An historical crisis is a period in which first principles that underlie a pattern of culture slowly die in the depths of collective consciousness. The relentless criticism of experience gradually reveals their inaptness to cope satisfactorily with the problems of life. The world built on them is at the end of its tether.[3]

An obvious example may help us in this regard. If we consider as part of a past Christian culture the principles of the "Just War morality", such principles surely die now in the Christian collective consciousness when faced with the experience of the possible nuclear winter. In other words, an institution can so live in the midst of a certain "relentless criticism" that some of its principles, at least, reveal an "inaptness to cope satisfactorily with the problems of life". There may well be debate within the institution about such inaptness. In other words, some may say: "Our principles are as apt as ever"; and some may say the opposite. But the very fact of the debate itself demonstrates the presence of a crisis. Crises cannot be ignored. Some change, at least, is called for, and our minds must be at least open to the idea of a possible new future.

When I described my formation to the priesthood following upon my "going away", it was deliberately placed historically. I stepped onto the road to the priesthood after what is called the Second World War; I began my formation after the horror and terror of "The Holocaust"; my movement towards priesthood was in the years immediately after "The Bomb" had been exploded on Japan; and in the United Kingdom of those days, a whole new vision was awakening inspired by the establishment of the "Welfare State". Though there is a distinctive discipline to be pursued called "theology", it is amazing, when I look back, how little impact those events made upon that pursuit of theology. I could never so pursue theology now. And although, I am told, things are different in a "post-Vatican II" Church, I must admit to a certain degree of scepticism. This is not to denigrate the vast theological projects of a vast number of distinguished theologians, far from it. But the search for the immutable, with its predominance of "being" over "becoming", lies too heavily upon our understanding of God. In such a context, I believe that creativity and imagination, philosophically and theologically, find themselves oppressed by this concern with conservation. I am not unsympathetic with the sentiments of Claudel, who once wrote of the nineteenth century:

> The crisis which reached its most acute phase in the nineteenth century, was not primarily, an intellectual crisis ... I would prefer to say it was the tragedy of a starved imagination.[4]

The excitement to be found in so many theological projects of the recent past has simply not found its way into the spirituality of my contemporary brothers and sisters. We seem to be haunted by fear and anxiety, and – worse still – such a failure prepares the ground for a surrender to certain forms of respectable Christianity, which forms do no more than prop up the oppressive boredom of so much conservative, social, economic, political and cultural tendencies. Too many of us will not stand on new and unknown "junction platforms". If we do find ourselves on such platforms, we rush into the warmth and security of safe theological and philosophical "waiting rooms", only agreeing to come out and board that train which will carry us to already known and experienced destinations.

I will always treasure the past. It created me, but it cannot sustain me and it is in danger, when constantly repeated, of distracting me – even preventing me – from discovering new mediations of God.

CHAPTER THREE

A Reflection upon the Christian Roots of Power

A friend of mine recently remarked to me that she found it quite extraordinary that people of insight, not to mention people driven by the simplicity of the Gospel of Jesus, people of creativity and imagination, continued to seek power within the accepted ecclesiastical establishment. When I asked her what she meant she said that if people looked at the world in which we live, its agonies and its joys, its depressions and its hopes, they could surely see that ecclesiastical power never released creativity and imagination; the power of the Gospel so often made itself felt precisely in opposition to ecclesiastical power.

I am not without sympathy for such a view. It occupies my mind greatly these days. Of course the ecclesiastical establishment will always throw up the power-seekers, not because they are ecclesiastical people, but because they are simply people. They will dress up their quest for power with profound theological, not to say evangelical, motivations or they will say they are acting for the release of the creativity and imagination of others. One must cope with and temper them. At the same time, I must say I do not think things are quite that simple, but the question of power is vital, and we shall return to it.

There is a strange form of puritanism that creeps into Christian discussions about power. Francis of Assisi possessed and exercised power. Adolf Hitler possessed and exercised power. The origins of their power may have differed and their exercise of power may not bear comparison, not to mention the consequences of both its possession and exercise. Nevertheless, they both possessed and exercised power which they had taken up, or taken from, somewhere or someone. And there is a further complication. The people wanted them to have power and vicariously possessed and exercised it. This power was given to Francis and Hitler, not in some abstract way, but by other human beings. Power, and therefore powerlessness, may exist in differing degrees and modes, have differing causes and motivations. Power and powerlessness are facts of life.

Some years ago, I remember preparing for a class in philosophy. I came across this passage from Bertrand Russell:

Power over human beings may be classified by the manner of influencing individuals or by the type of organisation involved.
   An individual may be influenced:
   a) By direct power over his body, e.g., when he is imprisoned or killed;
   b) By rewards and punishments as inducements, e.g., in giving or witholding employment;
   c) By influence on opinion, i.e., propaganda in its broadest sense.
   Under this last head, I would include the opportunity for creating desired habits in others, e.g., military drill, the only difference being that in such cases action follows without any such intermediary as could be called opinion.
   These forms of power are most nakedly and simply displayed in our dealings with animals, where disguises and pretenses are not necessary. When a pig with a rope round its middle is hoisted squealing into a ship, it is subject to direct physical power over its body. On the other hand, when the proverbial donkey follows the proverbial carrot, we induce him to act as we wish by persuading him that it is in his own interest to do so. Intermediate between these two cases is that of the performing animals, in different ways, that of the sheep induced to embark on a ship, when the leader has to be dragged across the gangway by force, and the rest then follow willingly ... The case of the pig illustrates military and police power. The donkey with the carrot typifies propaganda. Performing animals show the power of education.[1]

In the examples of Russell we encounter a power that is physical, a power that is rooted in propaganda and a power motivated and caused by education. Why did I never use the quotation? I believe because I was bemused by it; what power as priests in the future were those students being given? Indeed, what power had I been invested with on the junction platform so many years ago? Certainly there is a definition of priest and priesthood, but those family friends on the platform were giving me *power*. They were endowing me with a place in life, and their motives were not unambivalent.

Last Holy Thursday, in the Christian calendar the day before Jesus suffered upon the Cross, I found myself in a very problematic spiritual mood. I entered a cathedral to participate in the "blessing of the holy oils". I found myself totally overcome by the "maleness" of the situation. I am sure many a woman has more profoundly gone through this experience before me. No matter how spiritual the moment may have been, no matter how moving the experience may have been of priests renewing their own givenness to God, the ethos of "man" dominated the situation I found myself in.

"Religion, or what societies hold to be sacred, comprises an institutionalised system of symbols, beliefs, values and practices focused on questions of ultimate meaning."[2] Christianity, and my own expression of Christianity, is an expression of this institutionalised system of symbols, beliefs, values and practices focused on questions of ultimate meaning. No matter how involved we may become, and indeed should become, in the struggle of humanity for fulfilment, the liturgical moment is the most radical expression of our depressions and hopes, our sorrows and joys.

Though that liturgical moment may well be centred upon or focused upon what we have inherited, it should surely also be an expression of the deepest struggles out of oppression in any given moment of history. In other words, there is a sense in which the expression of biblical and spiritual Christian liberation must reflect, even fulfil, the deeper struggle for human liberation. To put this in very biblical language, the Passover of Jesus translated into the Passover of the Christian Church must reflect the "human historical passover" of my brothers and sisters in this world. I found myself overwhelmed by the fact that ours was a male expression. This is not to play down, make little of or denigrate the struggles and hopes of my brother priests, but I cannot help but feel questions emerging in my soul about the location and exercise of male power. The drama of humanity seemed to be rooted in a male act of spiritual choreography.

The ever-present danger in the exercise of power is that it marginalises. Whatever the group or paradigm, the possession and exercise of power cannot be explained simply in terms of Russell's pig, donkey or performing animal. There is something much more subtle, yet no less oppressive, involved. It is the sense of "not being part of it". It is ultimately the sense of marginalisation. I feel we do not always quite grasp this fact. The situation becomes increasingly more depressive and oppressive when a discussion is initiated, leavened and bristling with all kinds of distinctions, focusing upon the question: "How shall we bring *them* out of the margins?" *They*, those "outside", simply become a "talking-point".

It would seem to me that moments of crisis do, from time to time, evoke creative and imaginative responses in any institution or establishment. They can also call forth highly oppressive responses.

> Persistent shortsightedness, selectivity and tolerated contradiction are usually not so much signs of perceptual weakness as signs of strong intention to protect certain values and their accompanying institutional forms.[3]

The responses, of whichever kind, are the manifestation of power. The history of the Church bears witness to both. It has experienced and been responsible for creativity and imagination, and I would think Vatican II is an example of this. But the root causes of the responses are not always found at the central point, or points, of power. But what does concern one is the slowness of response, the rather exaggerated expenditure of unnecessary emotional and intellectual energy involved in accepting a new "Clock of Influence". And even when a new "Clock of Influence" is accepted, there is a continuing failure to respond to the ecstatic and agonising word which comes from the *world* and the *human quest*.

When we speak of human relationships we sometimes give the impression that it is the world in which we live, the human quest in life we enter into, the culture which we inherit and in which we create those human relationships. This is one way of looking at life, but there is another way, and I feel it to be more and more important. I feel it would be better for us to see our social relationships as the creator of the world, the human quest and, indeed, of what we call culture. I, late twentieth-century man, am part of a whole web of human relationships. These may be marked by creativity, hope and fulfilment; they may also be marked by destruction and despair. And though there is a personal and individual uniqueness about the "I" that I am, I am born into, and live out my life within, a world of social relationships. It is from this energy that the world, the human quest and the culture of my life emerges. It emerges from this particular energy of human relationships, not only because of my "here and now", but also because such an energy has always been part of the evolution of humanity. It is an important part of my historical inheritance.

Christianity and the Church are also the result of the energy of social relationships. I am not suggesting in saying this that such an energy creates God or Christianity or Church. Indeed, one may argue that God, Christianity and Church are creative of distinctive relationships. For example, my Christian tradition mediates God to me and mediates a new format of relationships with my brothers and sisters in the world. There is also at the root of this latter dimension of my life an "act of belief". But the essential point is that the social relationships which create the world in which I live, the human quest of which I am a part and the culture to which I belong, are in themselves a mediation of God. This mediation is concretised in the world, in the human quest and in patterns of culture. In the varied human concretisations of these vast realities God is also to be sought. In my friendships of life, for example, I encounter God. Let me repeat that I am not saying God *is* the mediations or the mediations are God. Just as the Christian tradition is not God but the mode by which and in which God addresses me, so all the mediations I have spoken about are not God, they are God speaking a word to me and acting in my world. If I fail to honour such mediations I deprive myself of an enriching openness to the wonder of God's ever-revealing act. I also fail to see that what perverts humankind is evil, not because it blocks the wonder of "being human", but because God's creativity is in the process of destruction. For at the very roots of "being human" is God. This is vital in order that, among other things, I may develop with my brothers and sisters in this world a profound respect for the world in itself and a seriousness of commitment to a life of respect for the world and God in our social relationships.

So often today the liberation of the poor, the recognition of women in society, the understanding of racism and, indeed, the nuclear debate, seem to be removed from the "God" question. In particular, the struggle towards demarginalisation of all those who are stigmatised, alienated and marginalised, is not perceived as a profound question about a mediation of God at the centre of humanity's possession and exercise of power over destiny.

If the Christian Church of our times feels marginalised, as an institution, I feel now that this is so because the world and the human quest are too often perceived merely as "agencies" worth consulting. The wonder of everything gathered into a awe-inspiring mediation of God is not quite the starting point. The interaction and intermingling of Church, world and human quest does not seem to be a radical ground for living and conversing.

Two propositions are common coinage in certain circles today. One is, "The Church is too much into politics"; the other, "The Church has failed in its strong moral stand". Now I admit that the Church is a distinctive institution, and I further admit that it is called to work at a distinctive agenda. Taking the latter proposition first, there is a tendency for certain types of Christians, and indeed non-Christians, to suggest that because the Church has failed in its so-called strong moral stand, the world in general, and society in particular, is suffering a breakdown. Now I am not immediately disputing this view, but it is important to grasp that the breakdown is not because of an ecclesiastical failure or silence on moral matters. It must first be located in the failure of humanity itself to honour its own dignity and activate its own innate tendency to search for authentic fulfilment. In other words, society has ceased to understand what it is to be truly human. If religion in general, or the Church in particular, is to address such a society realistically and relevantly, the Church must recognise this energy that still thrives in human beings, even if those human beings are not part of, or even reject, the Church. The Church must see the world and the human quest as bearers of the mediations of God. In other words, we must recognise and identify God, with fortitude and clarity, in those movements of society which demonstrate the strivings, the struggles and the sufferings of humanity's quest for fulfilment. This means that we must see those movements as ministering to the Church if the Church's ministry to society is to have any relevance. This will often mean that we must move out of areas of morality that are predictable.

It has not been unknown in recent times for distinguished politicians to utter the proposition about the Church's failure to take a moral stand and, at the same time, when it highlights examples of dehumanisation and oppression which follow from certain political programmes, accuse the Church of political interference. If the Church is to counter such an argument, it must do so by reminding the same politicians that their programmes are leading society away from the fulfilment of its own quest for true human dignity, which for the Church is a mediation of God, and if it has not identified the very struggle for liberation, in certain oppressed sectors of society, as a mediation of God and absolutely essential to the understanding of God and the Gospel of Jesus, then its words within the political forum are hollow.

I am not suggesting that the Church has not officially spoken in such terms; that is, in terms of God moving in the life of humanity. One has only to recall certain words of Vatican II documentation. But I still ask myself how deeply this has penetrated the total life of the Church, which still seems enclosed and introspective. What seems necessary is not so much changes of structure, but a profounder understanding of the mediations of God as I have tried to describe them. There is a fear to review honestly the mode and nature of its possession and exercise of power within the world. The point I wish to make is that such a review cannot take place without a shift in our understanding of God's mediation and in our willingness to decide upon the priorities of our "Clock of Influence".

There has to be interaction between world and human quest on the one hand, and Christian belief and reflection on the other. Christian belief and reflection are not met by a dead and passive human spirit but by a spirit that is alive, seeking, conversing, anguishing about its vision and dreams. "There can be in the human spirit," wrote Frederick Copleston, the Jesuit and distinguished philosopher,

> a movement of transcendence which can take various forms. This movement effects entry into a dimension of experience in which the idea of divine reality makes sense. That is to say, it is the complement of the movement of the finite spirit. I do not claim that this sort of experience necessarily leads a man to use the *word* "God". He may not do so. But I doubt whether this is a matter of primary importance. Nor do I claim that these types of experience necessarily lead a man to assert the existence of a transcendent reality, whether he uses the word "God" or not. All that I claim is that there can be in the human spirit an opening, as it were, to the transcendent. At this point a man is faced with what is, from the empirical point of view, an option, the option that is to say, between affirming or denying the reality of the transcendent.[4]

But whether man recognises or refuses to recognise such transcendency, in my own vision, humanity's struggles and hopes are borne up, by that transcendency.

My own concern is not about the proof or demonstration of God's existence in this meditation. I have taken such a fact for granted. I do not make such statements to impose my view upon my contemporaries. Indeed, like Fr Copleston,

> I see no good reason for asserting its [the transcendent's] absence

or disappearance. To be sure, there are plenty of people who feel unable to accept what they regard as the traditional and paradigm concept of God. But that modern man is closed altogether to the transcendent seems to me a gratuitous assumption. Even in the most unpromising surroundings – in a society, for example, where atheism is officially taught and in which the young are indoctrinated with the view that religion is a thing of the past, not only outmoded but also socially harmful – an interest in religious problems, manifesting what I describe as the movement of transcendence, tends to reassert itself. Even in the modern world there are those for whom secular humanism is inadequate. They may not look to the Churches, but it does not follow that they are not open to God.[5]

I raise these points only to highlight my own deep concern at this stage of my priesthood, and Copleston's final sentence indirectly makes my point. I do not believe that the Church will ever come to a stage of presenting an apologetic for God until it makes the philosophical and theological, not to say spiritual, shift I have suggested, which consists in the profound acknowledgement that the struggles towards liberation in the world and in the contemporary human quest must be seen as major mediations of the living God.

Indeed, I would go further. Christianity, especially in its institutional existence, cannot be its true self, cannot define, or indeed validly describe, its power unless it sees its power as necessarily responsible to, and dependent upon, the living world and humanity's quest for its own fulfilment. The struggle for liberation and the never ceasing effort of so many human beings to love each other, even to the point of death, surrounded by oppression and hatred, are not consultative points for the institutional Church's apologetic on behalf of God. The institutional Church, if we look hard and long enough, may well discover in such mediations the authentic face of God.

I would be the first to admit that the world's struggles can be ambivalent. I am conscious of the absurdities, so often offered us as paths to reason and the violence imposed upon us as paths to peace, which slowly and relentlessly crush the little ones of this world. We can only enter on such a path of reflection

through seeing the world and human quest, especially in their
concrete manifestations, as God's mediations. The most concrete examples of such mediations, I believe, are the various
struggles for liberation from all marginalisation. I have already
attempted to make it clear that I treasure heritage and tradition
and historical content. But these treasured gifts must be made
to open my faith into a more exciting and, indeed, risk-laden
present, which can point into an unknown future. Stories of a
past, no matter how important, must have a distinctive meaning for a present.

> The anthropologist is not doing his job if he merely offers to teach
> us how to bicker with his favourite tribe, how to be initiated into
> their rituals, etc. What we want to be told is whether that tribe has
> anything interesting to tell us – interesting by *our* lights, answering
> to *our concerns*, informative about what we know to exist. Any
> anthropologist who rejected this assignment on the grounds that
> filtering and paraphrase would distort and betray the integrity of
> the tribe's culture would no longer be an anthropologist, but a sort
> of cultist. He is, after all, working for *us* not for *them*. Similarly,
> the historian of X where X is something we know to be real and
> important, is working for those of us who share that knowledge,
> not for our unfortunate ancestors who did not.[6]

As a priest and a religious – the latter I have yet to speak about,
but will shortly – I put myself in the position of that anthropo-
logist and historian. The demanding voice I hear today is the
voice of the powerless of this world calling in a debt from
religion and the Church. Their struggle is God's mediation. I
have yet to come to the point but the junction platform upon
which I heard and hear that voice is what is called Inner City.
There are many reasons for my not listening hard enough,
there are many reasons for my deafness and there are many
reasons for my escapism, but I so meditate because of my love
for and awareness of the creative energy still alive within the
Church and the religious life.

CHAPTER FOUR

The Golgotha Experience

It was a Sunday night in December. No wallflowers now, but a very country scene: a village church situated in the Cotswolds. I was requested to prostrate myself on the sanctuary floor of the church and as I lay there a priest read aloud the account of Jesus's suffering as recorded by the Johannine community, written close on two thousand years ago. I then made a vow, that for the rest of my life I would promote in the lives of those to whom I preached and with whom I worked a loving remembrance of Jesus's sufferings. It was a brilliantly staged set-piece of symbolism. For I could hear during this reading the tolling of the death bell. I was dying yet living; living yet dying. Forty and more years have neither dimmed the scene or muffled the tolling of that bell, and though ideals have crumbled, though hurt has come to others who have come into my life and passed on, though new horizons have arisen, there has been something unchangeable in my life which was rooted in that event. That night I became a Passionist. I became a member of a Roman Catholic religious order known as the Community of the Passion. The community was founded in the eighteenth century and came to England during that crucial period of English history, the mid-nineteenth century, at the height of what is now described as the Industrial Revolution. It has been my good fortune to remain part of that community, to argue in it and with it, to play some part in its development, to share its joys and sorrows, its hopes and despairs and to make a contribution, at the highest level of its decision-making, to its life and work. But I must make a confession: it has taken me over forty years to understand the significance of the symbolism of that December night.

The symbolism of dying and the symbolism of the reading of
Jesus's Passion are now beginning to make new sense to me.
The symbolism suggests a powerfulness of God rooted in a
tragic and terrible powerlessness. Let us for a moment consider
what religious symbolism means.

As I put letters together on these pages, the letters are
symbols of the words which they make up. But the words are
also symbols. They are the symbols of the meaning which I
wish to communicate to you. In other words, that which is
symbolised can also be a symbol.[1] The night, for example, on
which I joined my religious order I was given a crucifix. I still
possess it. The crucifix was first of all the symbol of an event
which took place two thousand years ago one Friday afternoon. The Hill of Golgotha upon which Jesus died on the
Cross, symbolised in my crucifix, is itself a symbol in Christian
belief of the action of God within history. But that action of
God within history is also a symbol of what ultimately
concerns humanity for it to achieve its fulfilment. What has
happened is something unseen or invisible, the fulfilment of
humanity, and has been made perceptible in the series of
symbols: deeper still, this whole series of symbols is saying
something about God. To take this a step further, the symbol
possesses an innate power in itself. Of course – and this is
crucial – none of this symbolism makes any sense at all unless
there is a social acceptance of it. In my case that social acceptance is tied up with my belief and the belief of other Christians.
But I would hope that even those who do not accept such
Christian belief may be able to interpret such symbolism in
terms of what contributes to human fulfilment and ultimate
meaning.

I say all this to make an essential point. In all our journeying
through life, leaving aside the philosophical and theological
agonising about the definition of God, our understanding of
and belief in God is caught up in a process of change. This
process of change is not simply rooted in my subjective responses, emotional or intellectual; the process is the result, too,
of the forces of history, social, economic, political and cultural,
to which I find myself subject.

No matter how many documents rule my life, no matter how many books I may read, no matter how many ideas I live by, the "conversation" I hold with the world in which I live, both locally and internationally, dictates my life. And if, as I do, I believe in God and understand the meaning of God to be symbolised by the suffering of Jesus, symbolised in its turn by my crucifix, so too does that "conversation" with my world shape my understanding of the God revealed and made flesh in Jesus. To put this another way, the Word made flesh in Jesus, the Word of God, is influenced by the words I exchange and perceive in the hopes and struggles of the world. If I believe certain hopes and struggles, joys and sorrows, are priorities in the world, such priorities will have a major effect upon my understanding of God.

The Christian conversation, both within the Christian community itself and with the world at large, must be forever influenced by anxieties and choices about such priorities. This means there is bound to be conflict and tension within the Christian community. For wherever women and men join in conversation there is bound to be opinion. To attempt to transcend such tension and conflict in the name of harmony is to destroy not only the development of the Christian community and the world, it is to destroy the very meaning of what it is to be human. Indeed it is to search for a false, and ultimately destructive, harmony. I understand tension to have a creative possibility. It ceases to be creative when it is emptied of mutual respect and radical honesty. Furthermore, uncreative tension never creates the context for love, be that love human or divine. A sure way of allowing ourselves to be uncreative is to become imprisoned by or to submit to an imprisonment in documents, no matter how noble and wonderful the documents may be.

On my desk at this moment there are four small books or documents. One is dated 1775, another 1934, the third carries the date 1962 and the fourth 1984. They are all copies of the Rule I was called to live by when I was accepted into the Community of the Passion that December night over forty years ago. I wish to quote two passages. One passage is from

the document I was given forty years ago, the other is from the
latest revision of that same document which was first written in
1968 and was finally published in 1984.

> Since, however, one of the chief objects of our Congregation is not
> only to devote ourselves to prayer, that we may be united to God
> by charity, but also to lead others to the same end, instructing
> them in the best and easiest manner possible; therefore those
> members who may be considered fit for so great a work, should
> both during apostolic missions and other exercises, teach the
> people by word of mouth to meditate devoutly on the Mysteries,
> Sufferings and Death of our Lord Jesus Christ, from Whom, as
> from a fountain, all our good proceeds.[2]

So reads an example of the theory and the practice of my
religious order as given to me when I was first received. But let
me now quote from the 1984 edition.

> We are aware that the Passion of Christ continues in this world
> until he comes in glory; therefore, we share in the joys and sorrows
> of our contemporaries as we journey through life toward our
> Father. We wish to share in the distress of all, especially those who
> are poor and neglected; we seek to offer them comfort and to
> relieve the burden of their sorrow.
> The power of the Cross, which is the wisdom of God, gives us
> strength to discern and remove the causes of human suffering.
> For this reason, our mission aims at evangelising others by
> means of the Word of the Cross. In this way all may come to know
> Christ and the power of his resurrection, may share in His suffer-
> ings and, becoming like Him in his death, may be united with him
> in glory. Each of us takes part in this apostolate according to his
> gifts, resources and ministries.[3]

In some ways one may say that both documents highlight the
same points, but in the latter documentation an anxiety makes
itself felt. This anxiety is rooted in the existence of the poor of
this world; there is also an anxiety expressed about the very
causes of human suffering.

The point I wish to make is this. It is not simply that within
the community I joined so long ago there was a rethink about
its own tradition. Of course, such a rethink took place, but a

word was spoken in our times and by our times about the powerless and the suffering of this world. This word was spoken by the world. A new mediation of God had taken place, a mediation revealed in the living obscenity of the oppressed. The debates which were part of such a rethink were not easy; I was part of them during the years 1968 to 1970. But one thing must be said: the community had not imprisoned itself in earlier documentation, though it had honoured it; it had also allowed itself to hear, in a liberating conversation, as all true conversation must be, the cry of the poor.

In the early 1950s I was ordained a Roman Catholic priest. That occasion was full of symbolism. But there was a subtle difference in the symbolism. In my profession, that act of dying which I have spoken about, I was offered a sense of the powerlessness of God in which powerlessness paradoxically there rested power; in my ordination to the priesthood I felt I had been given power. To be sure, it can be said that such a power rested in the power of the sacraments, especially of the Eucharist. I treasure such a thought, but life's experience has brought confusion. It is a confusion which questions not the reality of the priestly life of the Church, but the clerical life of the Church. I am not passing judgement, but I do feel a certain unease. The unease concerns the external symbolism of the clerical life which enjoys a position, a social status and a form of social acceptability which, though not destroying the power of God's mediation, becomes a distraction in a world struggling for a new understanding of liberation.

To raise a question about the mode of existence of any group, of any institution or of any social order, is not to deny the existence of the group or the institution or a social order. If I say, for example, that the theology of suffering can never be the same again after the experience of Auschwitz, or that the understanding of sinfulness must be re-examined after the horror of the struggle for liberation by the black peoples of our world, I am denying neither a theology of suffering nor the reality of sinfulness. I am calling rather for new horizons and suggesting other "junctions" for the Christian journey.

To approach life in this way is not to dishonour God, it is

rather to give homage and worship. God may look into the eternal mirror, so to speak, and gaze upon an image of unchangeableness. If I look into my temporal mirror of history and gaze upon changeableness, and if that changeableness forces me to bring to bear upon God new insights about his existence and action, I am doing no more than acknowledging my participation in God's creativity. My struggling efforts at redefining or redescribing God are the manifestation of the creativity and imagination bestowed upon me by God.

There can be a terrible arrogance about one's view of the Church. The arrogance can rest in our endowing it with an unchangeableness which denies the very same creativity of God. Of course, one must have a mind for a teaching authority. This mindfulness does not dispense me from directing the gaze of such an authority towards the new horizons. Furthermore, on the negative side, if I believe there are new and major areas of sinfulness in our world and in our human quest, which in their turn offend against the wonder of the God of all goodness, then to present these is also to honour God and recognise the power of his revelation.

Because of the religious grouping to which I belong, namely the Community of the Passion, all my functions in life will be dominated by a God, theoretically and practically, mediated in the event of Golgotha. But that event is not mine alone. I would suggest it belongs to a whole world, no matter how variously it may be interpreted. But in our world, in which the contrast of power and powerlessness has become so apparent, Golgotha has an even deeper relevance.

This is not a programme for a spirituality of morbidity. It is rather to suggest that that historical junction has the makings of a contemporary junction in all our journeying. It is a profound reminder summoning us all to a new self-emptying. That self-emptying must find its ways not only into theological interpretations of life, but also into a new understanding of our political, social, economic and cultural ideologies and structures. Church and State must find new vision and, therefore, a new symbolism or an old symbolism revised. This is no easy agenda. We cannot escape the experience and reality of Gol-

gotha, though I feel that far too many of us try to do so, and so
live out a life of unhealing reform and increasing inhumanity. I
believe a revolution is called for, based upon the Golgotha
experience.

When it comes to memory we are all victims of selectivity.
But the ultimate sin would be to select from the past only those
things which protect the contemporary "*status quo*".

Such a philosophy not only destroys the authentic past, it
also destroys the present; and thus prevents that present from a
true openness to the future. "Rule Britannia" and "God bless
the Pope" have, I am sure, valid cultural contributions to offer,
but in themselves they will not create a future State of nobility
or Church of holiness. Both Britannia and the papacy are not
without sins to confess before God. The recognition of past
failure and present shortcoming are essential.

Authentic memory can enrich the present in which we live
and the future we seek to make a realistic possibility. As
Chenderlin has so ably put it:

> This is the very core of true historical – and memorial – thinking
> and living. The past retains its dignity while it blends with present
> experience.[4]

It is also important not to seek a past which underplays that
which is, so to speak, a harsh remembering. Though I believe,
as one captivated by the wonderful hopefulness of the risen
Jesus and whilst in my faith in, and understanding of, God I
must express hopefulness, I cannot make the horror of the
execution of Jesus a merely unfortunate event or a necessary
passageway for the glory of his rising. I must look at the death
of Jesus, contemplate the death of Jesus, for its own sake.
"Every time, then, you eat this bread and drink this cup, you
proclaim the death of the Lord until he comes."[5] Note that
stress upon "the death of the Lord". I must do this because it is
his death in the first instance, not his rising, which brings me to
the reality of his actions, actions which were offensive and
threatening to the religious establishment of his day. The
suffering of Jesus must always be a unique focus of my contem-

plation. The remembering of Jesus's execution must "retain its
dignity" and significance, "while it blends with present
experience".

Furthermore, the nature and act of Jesus's execution and
death must not be so gathered up into a universality of world
redemption that we lose the existential concreteness of the
execution and death in themselves.

To put this another way: Though one may agree that behind
the life of Jesus there is, so to speak, a contractual agreement
with his Father, his final response flowed from the fact that he
refused, though a faithful Jew, to accept the interpretation of
Yahweh by the religious establishment and the oppression of
the political establishment of his day. If we say that the host of
Heaven was witness to his agony, it is good to remember that
on the day of his execution there would be something in the
region of, approximately, 125,000 pilgrims in the city in addi-
tion to the city population of around 55,000. When he drew
fire from the temple establishment, he was confronting not
only the reigning high priest, but also the temple overseers, the
temple treasurers, the temple police, 7,200 priests, 9,600
levites, not to mention the colonial occupying power of Rome
and its upper class Hellenistic collaborators.

To be sure, such historical facts may be open to dispute and
some may rightly say they are not necessary for "my believing", but if my believing is to be of a piece with my living in my
present, it seems to me that they are not unhelpful as I search
for both the negative and positive concretisations of God's
mediation in the world in which I live. One cannot afford – the
Church cannot afford – to escape the existential and historical
memory of Golgotha, if it wishes to develop a spirituality and a
mission of credibility. There is a sense in which the statement
of "being all things to all men and all women" is to be found
rooted, when it comes to belief in God, in an option for a
transcendental philosophy and theology which never really
splashes down in the real ocean of human suffering. Or, when
there is a "splash-down", it is morally and spiritually predictable. One is reminded of those words from Robert Bolt's play,
A Man For All Seasons: "It is not hard to stay alive, friends, just

don't make trouble. And when you do, make sure it is the kind
of trouble they expect of you."

Remembering Jesus's execution and death, then, is a harsh
remembering; and if it is heavenly bound, it is also earthly
rooted. The philosopher, Alfred Whitehead, wrote:

> The art of free society consists first in the maintenance of the
> symbolic code; and secondly in fearlessness of revision, to secure
> those purposes which satisfy an enlightened reason. Those socie-
> ties which cannot combine reverence to their symbols with free-
> dom of revision, must ultimately decay either from anarchy, or
> from the slow atrophy of a life stifled by useless shadows.

I have already talked about symbols within the context of a
very important event in my own personal life. Reverence for
those symbols remains deep in my life. But as other influences
have been brought to bear, so I look at those symbols in a new
way. The symbolism of my December day, when I was pre-
sented with the crucifix and pronounced a specific vow,
remains crucial for my life. Let me recall the fact that this
symbolic moment was also perceived as symbolic of God's
action within history. And that action within history was a
defining factor in my understanding of God. But if my own
community now broadens its understanding of the Passion of
Jesus, linking that suffering with the horror of the powerless in
this world, then the whole symbolic process takes on a new
meaning. For me that new meaning has been concretised by my
Inner City experience. Thus it can happen that the meaning of
the symbol may remain and yet, simultaneously, acquire a
whole new dimension. There is a sense, then, in which reverence for the symbol remains, but revision has taken place. In
such a situation it is not a question of the symbols being
perceived in a new way as isolated realities, it is rather that,
because of new mediations, the philosophy, the theology or
the vision behind them has undergone change.

I sense a confusion within the Church of my times. This
confusion results from a certain schizophrenic attitude to
vision and symbol: there is either an acceptance of a new

vision, but symbols remain unrevised or symbols undergo revision but the vision remains unchanged; or, which is even more confusing, it remains only superficially accepted.

The Church cannot, it would seem to me, establish symbols which seem to speak of a new Church of shared discipleship and equality and yet continue to hold on to an unrevised hierarchical symbolism. I am not denying the reality of a hierarchical Church: rather, I am questioning the symbolism of such a hierarchical situation.

I am, too, more than aware of being on very dangerous ground in such a reflection, but I believe the ground is only dangerous because we have remained too attached to interpretations of Christian power which have marginalised the major source of authentic Christian power. Christian power has been too quick to accept both the vision and the symbols of the inherited social, economic, political and cultural power, paradigms of our pyramidally organised world. In other words, if we have been given a dying God, a serving God, a God of the powerless, then we have access to a new understanding of power. By not so believing and acting we have, paradoxically, brought about the death of our true God by turning our backs upon the meaning and message of the true death of God. One should not be able to contemplate the naked body of Jesus sagging in death upon the Cross, a Jesus we believe to be God, without seriously asking questions about the meaning of power in the inherited symbol of Jesus, namely, the Christian community. If I know, as opposed to believe, that such a death was brought about because of institutional confrontation and oppression, religious and political, then for all time I am challenged by a quest concerning the meaning of Jesus and, *a fortiori*, God.

I am also called to a need for vital vigilance concerning the meaning of religious and political power and the dangers, ever present, of compromising that power in the face of more political and respectable paradigms of power. If I do not confront such questions, even if I never cease to believe in God, I am in grave danger of manipulating God or allowing other powers to manipulate God. Such manipulation is tantamount to an act of disbelief in God. This I believe to be a particularly problematic situation in groups, communities, societies and even nations which claim to be Christian and bury their loved ones with Christian symbols. The power of the Resurrection is utterly meaningless when detached from the distinctive powerlessness of Golgotha. If we wish to contemplate both events together, they must, nevertheless, be regarded as distinct events with distinct and empowering messages.

This empowering leads me to choose new dependencies in life. I am called into the centre of a living paradox. And that living paradox must give me a new and original confidence. The new dependency is the vision of the Gospel and, indeed, the vision of the Old Testament prophets. The power of God must be seen revealed, negatively and positively, in the powerless. Thus the paradox is that powerlessness is defined as power and power is powerlessness. I must search for the mediation of God in the cry of the powerless and in the struggle of the powerless for liberation. My confidence, a new-found confidence, must be my solidarity with that cry and that struggle. And, indeed, wherever and however I find oppression, marginalisation and stigmatisation, there I must find the voice of God. Golgotha, and the God of Golgotha, must lead me into the heartland, wherever that may be, the Inner City of today or the Belsen of yesteryear, not to find, in the first instance acts of courage to admire, but the horrific oppressions of humanity over humanity. Admiration may follow and, indeed, I will be empowered by the fortitude of many, but if I am to redefine power in this world I must contemplate, if possible "exist with, suffer with and act with", the naked reality of those who cry out for liberation. This holds out to me a new confidence. It is the confidence rooted, as Dietrich Bonhoeffer once put it, in

> an experience of incomparable value to have learned to see the great events of the history of the world from beneath: from the viewpoint of the useless, the suspect, the abused, the powerless, the oppressed, the despised – in a word, from the viewpoint of those who suffer.[6]

To escape Golgotha is to escape from this new, though

demanding, new confidence and take on the ever-increasing and superficial confidence of those who manipulate God in the name of a self-destructive and self-serving possession and exercise of power. Such confidence, which enthrones competition, ownership, privatised success, freedom without social demands and control of others without moral responsibility, is seductive. In terms of human development it is also ultimately naive. It is this naive confidence, sometimes sustained by impressive speculations which confuse this "question mark" planted on Calvary and which seems to say to us: *I am nothing of what you say*. The kenosis which is the issue in the Letter to the Philippians is something totally different from a beautiful metaphor. Lacking style, suppressing all pompous speech which we would think more worthy of the Lord, it turns us away from our ordinary way of speaking and thinking. It invites us not indeed to an abstract meditation on negation and negativity, but to a renunciation, to an operative negation which should change our hearts and spirits. The Greek term *metanoia* expresses the essence of this conversion very well; it is a transformation, a change of spirit which frees us, through a certain death, from a common sense shared by far too many.

CHAPTER FIVE

The God of Golgotha

The God who came to dominate my life in my teenage years, and throughout my adult life, has been the God of Golgotha. The Christ of suffering, the suffering servant, has been the hinge of all my thought and prayer. I was trained as a very young man to meditate upon such a God and given a vision of life and action which would be about communicating such a God to others.

For all those years I have no regret either for such a philosophy of life or for training in such a philosophy of life. The suffering Christ at the centre of my life has served me well and enriched me beyond words, but now in later years I am beginning to understand the significance of that spirituality in a new way. Indeed, I have suggested already that I feel I am only now coming to understand Golgotha as an event and symbol leading to a distinctive understanding of God. I am only now coming to understand the path I specifically entered upon over forty years ago in terms of my understanding and service of God.

Death is not only, or indeed immediately, the ultimate sign of life's end game. It is also a reminder of our radical weakness and contingency. I feel concerned in these days about a certain fear of weakness and contingency. Perhaps it is to do with so much war, so much famine and, indeed, that collective consciousness of the possibility of a nuclear winter. That, however, is the global agenda. I am thinking of matters much more simple, though no less tragic and demanding. It appears to me that the powerless and the weak of this world too often find themselves perceived and described as the cause of their own weakness and powerlessness. We hide our broken in mind and spirit from our daily perception. On a very prosaic level, one at times feels one must apologise for illness and ageing in a jogging, youthful world. Speaking now in Christian terms, I feel this fear of gazing upon and reaching for, indeed putting at the centre of life, our powerless and marginalised fellow human beings, flows from our failure to understand God in terms of the weakness of Golgotha. The suffering and dying God is dubbed a *sine qua non* of resurrection, to which we can't get quickly enough. But this underpins not a theology of the resurrection but a superficial ideology of hope. And such an approach too often permits certain forms of political and social philosophy to manipulate God. I believe this to be the situation today in the United Kingdom. The situation is trivialised, philosophically and theologically, by undefined labels of "Left" and "Right".

There is an absurdity about the death of Jesus. I need to face this and understand it. Why should a good man die in such a barbarous way? Before outlining vast theologies of redemption, before talking about the world's sinfulness, indeed before talking about the wonder of the Resurrection and the foundation of a Church, we should contemplate the absurdity of that event. In other words, as I have already suggested, we should see very positive reasons for not escaping from Golgotha. If we do not so contemplate and assimilate, we shall never understand humanity's inhumanity and we shall never see the powerless, the weak and the marginalised of this world revealing a mediation of God, a mediation, I repeat, both negative and positive, challenging us to face a new, self-emptying action. I believe that Golgotha can lead us to an ecumenism deeper than the ecumenism of religious dialogue, which is central to our contemporary theological agenda. It is an ecumenism in which the human spirit reaches for the human spirit through an understanding of the blasphemy implied in oppressing and being oppressed.

An open contemplation of the death of Jesus, leading to a mystical union with God, leads us to examine the depth of our assimilation of, and relationship to, the values of Jesus. It often seems that it is only at the death of something or someone that we come to understand, in any depth, our relationship with that something or someone.

Let me linger for a moment upon Christian revelation in this regard. It is true that I find union with God in a new way through the Resurrection of Jesus. And, it is equally true, this union implies new values by which and with which I must live. But it is in the death of Jesus that I find very distinctive dimensions of those Christian values. Indeed, I discover their very roots in terms of his life as a preacher, a wandering rabbi and a protester against contemporary interpretations of Yahweh. Jesus did not say belief and hope in Yahweh, as taught him from childhood, were wrong. He claimed that the interpretations were wrong and too many of the interpreters had compromised God's covenant with his people. Many of them had collaborated not only with colonising powers on the political level, but also upon the theological level. They had accepted Hellenistic values, both politically and culturally; these values had corrupted the meaning of faith in Yahweh. He was claiming an authenticity rooted in the prophets. Such a discovery offers some insight into how Jesus came to die: he was a threat to the establishment of his day. I say all this to make but one point. It is this: if Jesus died in the cause of certain values, if those values are the roots of my believing, then the nature of my relationship to the execution and death of Jesus is vital.

I am not, as a Christian, concerned here with what I may see as the further claims of Jesus. Those further claims do not in any way affect the radical conduct of Jesus which resulted in suffering, trial, execution and death. They may well have increased the seriousness of the situation in which he found himself when faced by his own religious establishment; but this does not take away from the distinctive significance of his trial, execution and death. In the last analysis, I am suggesting that a contemplation and understanding of his suffering lead me to questions about his values and, consequently, about my relationship with those values. As I have said, it is the death of someone which leads one to question the nature, the quality and the depth of one's relationship with that person. If that person is a God who suffers, then I would think I have to struggle with a very profound definition of God. Whilst in terms of God this should not lead me to a consecration of suffering, it should lead me to a philosophy, not to say a theology, of suffering located realistically and radically in the paradigms of contemporary suffering, whether physical, social, political, economic, cultural or spiritual.

It is the motives and the values of Jesus which underpinned those motives, above all his identity with the powerless, which lift his death out of the realm of absurdity. But even at a deeper level still the absurdity is vanquished in that his dying, as well as his rising, is saying something about God. In a word, the suffering of Jesus carries not only a message about humanity, it carries a message about God. I have been struck by these words of Leonardo Boff concerning the absurdity of the Cross. I quote at length.

> Absurd as the cross is, it is still more absurd for God to have taken it up ... Absurd as it was for God to assume the cross, this constituted no obstacle for God. God is so great, so utterly beyond any possible negation, that God can understand to assume the absurd – not to divinise it, not to eternalise it, but to reveal the dimensions of divine glory, which transcend all light coming from the human logos and all darkness arising from the human heart.
>
> God assumes the cross in solidarity with and love for the crucified of history, with those who suffer the cross. God tells them, "absurd as it is, the cross can be the pathway of a marvellous liberation. But you must take it up in freedom and love. Then you will deliver the cross from its absurdity, and yourself from yourself. You are greater, and you become greater, than the cross. For liberty and love are greater than all absurdities, and stronger than death."[1]

It's so hard to let go, isn't it? I mean we have a rather inflated view of our own necessity. I mention this because it sums up another junction in my life. I was taken by ambulance one day from the prison (where I was working as a chaplain) to an outside hospital, with a suspected heart attack. It was a crucial event in my life. Indeed the state of health I have been left with has changed my life. It was, though I didn't particularly analyse it at the time, a very big junction in my life. I remember that night wondering about dying. I became, to myself, so necessary and, I would think, drew the suspect conclusion of being so necessary to everyone else. I remember reflecting during those days that all things come to an end. It is a fact so hard to take in, still less enthusiastically accept. Of course, it is essential for the survival of the human spirit that one should not just surrender – and, God knows, our greatest inspirers in life are those who have battled on in spite of so many odds against them; indeed, the powerless and the marginalised, the physically and mentally disabled people, some of whom I live with, are my daily resurrection.

But this non-acceptance of both is found at a more general level. We seem to find it impossible to admit that certain systems, structures, institutions, totalities, absolutes and abstractions have actually perished. This problem affects both the Church and the State and, because we cannot admit to such a dying, we do violence both to what we will not let go and to ourselves; indeed, we block the possibility of new dawnings. To deny the inevitable death of certain ideologies and structures is to enter upon a path of violence. Self-serving ideological transplants into the body ecclesiastical or politic seem to obsess us, when we should simply call it a day.

I should make it clear here that I am not supporting a view of truth, beloved of the pragmatists, which seeks to deny validity on the grounds that it does not work. To offer a practical political example: we cannot deny that the just redistribution of wealth is a true requirement for a noble society, because certain brands of socialism have not worked. And, indeed, we cannot deny the truth of the need to bend to wash the feet of the marginalised because the Gospel injunction hasn't yet been followed. That would be absurd. I am simply saying that things do die. Certain absolutes, ideas, abstractions, totalities, systems, do come to an end. The sun does set in life, physically and philosophically. As the little girl, sent to bed, and looking out on a beautiful sunset once said: "Well, if it must come to an end it couldn't happen more beautifully." But being sent to bed was an inevitability – it had to be faced and there had been no possible escape from the command.

To be sure, it is important that what is buried is buried gracefully, after due consideration and consultation, but the burial must take place. I have witnessed, and I am sure I am not alone, hours of emotional and intellectual energy expended upon efforts to keep alive that which cannot but be declared, often through nobody's fault, theologically, politically and socially dead. I say through nobody's fault but simply because new priorities in the relationships of the mediations or points on the "Clock of Influence" have emerged. Despite a flood of "second" opinions, engendering anxieties, guilt feelings and procrastination, the first diagnosis was accurate.

All death, whether in literal or analogical terms, implies grief and bereavement. Sometimes these two terms are used interchangeably, but they are quite distinct. Bereavement is about the actual state of loss or deprivation; grief concerns an emotional response. Beneath that response, however, there is a state of anxiety. If a very close friend of mine dies, for example, I face bereavement and I face grief. This is not only to be expected, it is even to be hoped for. But underlying my grief there is also a sense of anxiety. If that friend has meant a great deal to me and I have depended upon him or her, there is bound to be anxiety. And it is supremely important, if the loss is deep, that I face this or I am brought to face this by others. Above all things I must not be allowed to escape from the anxiety by pretending it is not really there, or by switching the anxiety away from myself to an anxiety for the one who is dead or to others suffering the grief and bereavement. The process must be carefully and painfully gone through, not brushed away by so-called commonsense statements, such as "time will heal", "we all have to die" and so forth. I am called at such moments to face up to the unbearable both in the objective loss and the subjective responses of grief and anxiety.

Bereavement, then, brings grief, and the grief has roots in anxiety about myself. There is nothing to be ashamed of in this.

But I must not live with the illusion that it may not have happened or that the friend will come back. I may for a while live with old memories, which will forever remain precious and treasured. But they must be maturely stored away. I must face the death and face myself and slowly come back into a real world now deprived, for me, of one close friend. I must come away from my anxieties; I must replace the anxieties which have flowed from my bereavement with other broader and more living anxieties; I must discover a new confidence. This is no easy task when life presents us with it, but when it does I must work all the way through it.

There is an analogy here with institutional Christianity, where the need for structural and theological change, which means the death of certain structures and theoretical stresses, brings about a certain bereavement and grief. I can understand this. But when one gets down to the anxiety beneath it all, I am inclined to believe that it is not truly confronted. One hears such questions and statements as, "Certain things never change", in "Where will the Church be without such and such a thing?" or "How can there be a future without this and that?" and "It's all a matter of fads and trends" and "The pendulum is going to swing back" – one could repeat them *ad nauseam*. God knows, I have talked like that myself, but deep down I am now inclined to believe that the real anxiety is about the self facing a new era, new beginnings, risk-laden paths and, more simply, a disturbed life.

We brush aside the possibility of an unbearable God, because we will not face up to the fact that new movements have brought about new mediations of God and new understandings of God. At the root of it all there is an unwillingness to face a Golgotha God, now in the form of a message which tells us that many of our structures, systems, totalities, theories and institutional modes, humanly and temporally crafted to carry divinely and eternally uttered words and truths, are dead or dying. *They must be allowed to die and be buried for there to be an authentic resurrection.* If this does not take place we not only turn away from the reality of the Golgotha God, we create illusionary expressions of the Resurrection of Christ. It is not that the death event or experience is simply a corridor to a future. Rather one must confront it and let it address the depths of the soul.

I would not want to be understood as being careless with inherited systems, structures, abstractions, totalities or absolutes. Far from it. For example, there is a system of law in every state and that system is a symbol of socially accepted obligations and responsibilities; there is a structure of democratic government which is also a symbol of social and political relationships. We use an abstract word like "community" which, when concretised, creates a mode of living together which, in its turn, is a symbol of people sharing interests and commitments. We speak in a language which communicates totalities: for example, "the State" or "the Nation" which also express symbolically a world of relationships and values; finally, we use terms like "law" and "order", which indicate the values underlying our communal life.

I will return to Church questions, but I have deliberately chosen the above examples because they have shaped many of our Christian symbols. I am not suggesting that we get rid of what has been historically inherited because we either become fed up with it or because it is under siege. But I am suggesting first, that we as human beings constructed these realities and that, therefore, they are not immortal; and second, that we always need to be careful that we do not hold on to them simply because they have been historically inherited, refusing at the same time to examine or discern the need for radical change in the face of new historical moments and movements. If we take such a road of intransigence it will lead us into violence. In other words, violence does not have to be immediately located in movements which challenge inherited symbols; violence can have its roots in a spiritual and intellectual stubbornness which resists all change and revision.

At a deeper level I am attempting to say that the resistance to change and revision, or the acceptance of change and revision, are to be seen flowing from a distinctive spirituality which, in Christian terms, I believe can be defined in the vision of the dying God. Such a dying in the face of "things" demands a mature and deliberate acceptance of death. One needs to see in death a distinctive value. Resistance all too often points to a desire, if not a panic, to hold on to an unhealthy form of stability and security which, though grounded in understandable anxiety, prevents development and liberation.

CHAPTER SIX

The Logic of the System and the Logic of Experience

It is good for us to remind ourselves of something too often forgotten. This point has already been made implicitly or, at least, hinted at. The death of Jesus was, in his own day, concerned with institutional and structural change. In other words, Jesus, a faithful Jew, was saying to his contemporaries that certain structures and institutional modes of existence and action must come to an end. To be sure, his vision was an ending that meant a new becoming. But the way "things" were, not only the way people were, had to change. Therefore a death experience had to be faced up to. As Dermot Lane has written: "There can be no doubt the journey up to Jerusalem by Jesus was a very significant, deliberate and conscious decision."[1]

I would not wish to suggest that Jesus envisioned no institutional future in terms of his own message and mission. To do so would be to undermine the significance of the Church to which I belong and in which I find my life. In other words, the confrontational opposition in the life of Jesus to the institutions of his day does not imply a vision which rejected an institutional future for his own community. But I do wish to suggest that the development of his message and mission has suffered from a search for development, security and progress which confuses the inner demands of the Gospel and the institutions which protect and prosper that Gospel, so that we sometimes find ourselves so highly protective of the symbols, the systems, the structures and the institutions that we confuse the inner message with the symbol of the message.

An example of this is to be found in priesthood. This seems to me to lead us to an unwillingness to "let go" in the name of a different future. Another example, affecting my own life, is that of the timidity expressed when faced with the need for a new or different expression of religious life. But – what is much more problematic – there can be the danger of not allowing a mediation of God, revealed in the experience of humankind, what I have called the human quest, to address my life. This is particularly dangerous when that mediation of God emerges from some of the deepest feelings of the human spirit. And there can be a further complication: without any malicious intent, I can unconsciously appear to be underpinning the *status quo* of society, when in fact that *status quo* must be challenged. In other words, when humankind is actually being summoned to let go of some of its own systems, structures, institutions, absolutes, not to mention some of its inherited certitudes, I can appear to be upholding them or supporting them.

I believe this to be a particularly troubling question of our times, namely that the logic of experience is subordinated to the logic of the system. In making such a statement I am not denying the need for system and I am not saying that the system should be subordinated to experience. Rather I am suggesting that, after discerning what is right and true for human development, we should make sure that systems are not protected in such a way that they obstruct it. This may all seem to be stating the obvious, but it does seem to me that we are unwilling to go deep enough in our attempt to discern the spirit of God historically at work in the human quest. To do so demands a profound respect for human experience.

It also demands the interiorisation of the Golgotha God. The more I meditate upon this in my own life and the more I look into the life of the Church, its priesthood and the religious life, the more attractive particular Gospel passages become. The anxiety expressed in our time by many Christians concerning our emphasis upon and research into the historical Jesus and his humanity must be treated with deep sensitivity and understanding. At the same time, it is important to remember that the Christian community is rooted in the human experiencing of Jesus by a group of his friends or disciples. Accepting the Gospels as integral for authentic Christian tradition and, therefore, fundamental to our act of believing, we must also see them as so many perspectives of Jesus's life, attempting to discern from these faith documents the human situation in which Jesus found himself and the human experience in which he sought the will of the one he called "Abba", Father. Jesus should not be seen as simply acting out a script which he had already read, going through a predetermined series of emotions which were not unexpectedly encountered, but rather "waited for".

The obedience of Jesus to the Word of the Father must be seen in the mediations of Jesus's life. Without any sophisticated or laboured exegesis the Gospel narratives introduce us to a Jesus invoking human experience, his own and his hearers, to highlight God's intervention in a day-to-day process. The birds of the air, the lilies of the field, the anxiety and care about tomorrow's needs, the harvest, the greed of the gluttonous, the riches of the powerful, the oppression of the religious establishment, his own tears at a friend's death, and his anxiety at his own imminent execution and death – a whole world, cosmologically and psychologically, he saw as a mediation of, or in opposition to, the word of God. Human experience as a source for understanding God and as a way to God is not the invention of contemporary theologians, it is a crucial part of the life and pedagogy of the God made flesh. For this very reason God's word is so often caught up in life's ambiguities. And like the whole of life God can be either bearable or unbearable.

To be sure, one must not romanticise either suffering or anxiety in Jesus, for it is important that we be liberated from suffering and anxious moments; but seeing such experiences as a road to a deeper understanding of God and humanity is vital. To accept in such experiences the actual word of God, no matter how unbearable it may appear, in the cause of human deliverance must be at the heart of one's life's journeying. Experience, my own or that of my suffering brothers and sisters, may teach me: "The day is done. You must allow a new dawning and lay to rest certitudes which can serve you no more, structures which will only lead to oppressions."

In this there is one Gospel passage to which I now go time and time again.

Among those who went up to worship at the Festival were some Greeks. These approached Philip, who came from Bethsaida in Galilee, and put this request to him, "Sir, we should like to see Jesus." Philip went to tell Andrew, and Andrew and Philip together went to tell Jesus.

Jesus replied to them: "Now the hour has come for the Son of Man to be glorified. I tell you most solemnly, unless a wheat grain falls on the ground and dies, it remains only a single grain; but if it dies, it yields a rich harvest. Anyone who loves his life loses it; anyone who hates his life in this world will keep it for eternal life ... Now my soul is troubled. What shall I say: Father save me from this hour? But it was for this very reason that I have come to this hour. Father, glorify your name."[2]

Did the possibility of talking to these Greeks tempt Jesus into extending his ministry? Did he see here a chance to appeal to a different constituency? Did he feel like a man or woman cut off at the height of a mission which he wished to prolong? Whatever the answers may be, there was an experience telling him to let go, face the final confrontation which, quixotic as it was, would lead to execution and death. He accepted the unbearable summons to powerlessness. But his decision arose not simply out of hearing the voice of the Father in his troubled soul. His interpretation of that voice came out of an accumulative experience leading him to the final act of his life. In Jesus's journey it was the vital junction.

I look at my own life and at the life of the Church in these days and I enquire into this progressive surrender to powerlessness, by attempting to redefine power, for the sake of the powerless. What I have called the logic of the system so often finds reasons to reject the logic of experience. By so doing we create and live with artificial, though seductive, symbols of Resurrection. To give a concrete example: thousands attending, perhaps returning to, Church life, thousands attending

Church congresses, may well be interpreted as symbols of the Resurrection, but they may also be artificial – indeed, they are affirming the logic of the system. Yet the cry of the powerless of this world heard and responded to as the voice of God may be a more authentic voice of God. This may upset certain respectable and comfortable aspects of the system, may challenge the premises of the logic of the system, but in the long run this logic of experience will create a new world by creating a new logic of the system. This is not a question of denying anything, it is rather a question of enrichment. I believe it was Martin Luther King who once said: "If a man has nothing to die for he has nothing to live for."

One cannot liberate the powerless of this world without radically changing the powerful.

What I have called the logic of experience has been the vital ingredient, so to speak, in all my junctions in life. I should think this to be the case for anyone. God did not come to dominate my life by way of a system, even the system of the Church. My parents' living love brought God to me. Thus in gathering me as a child into their arms, I was gathered into God. The Church as system and institution did not bring me to that junction so long ago; it was the living experience of certain people who came into my life. And though that December day, when I was asked to commit myself to an understanding of the Golgotha God in a very pertinent way, may well have depended upon the logic of a system, it was the living experience, conscious and unconscious, of others which was crucial. I would think it was the same when I entered the Roman Catholic priesthood within my religious community. It goes without saying that my experience may well have been rooted in a logic of a system, namely, the institutional Church. As I have said, God's mediation in my life has been through the institutional Church, in which I live as a religious and priest, and in which I continue to find God. But at this stage of my life I have become much more reverential towards and respectful of the logic of life, which flows from human experience, even in terms of my commitments as priest and religious. It is a fact of human living, whatever order we choose to consider, that there must be a human experiencing, with its own distinctive modes of thought and expression, before there can ever be a system, with its own distinctive modes of thought and expression. This is what I mean by the logic of experience and the logic of the system.

It is also a fact of human life that both logics will very often find themselves in opposition. Such opposition can be very healthy. The crucial point is that the oppositions must be worked out: they cannot be ignored without the consequences of chaos, anarchy or oppression.

All the great ventures of life begin in human experience. Certain human experiences are organised, they are structured and they are institutionalised: in a word, human experience becomes systematised. The tragedy is that in such systematisation the richness of the human experience can be sacrificed to the smooth running of the system. Thus some of the good of the initial experience is maintained, but a great deal is lost. More often than not, opposition simmers within the system which leads either to the death of the system because people abandon it, or to the overthrow of the system; or, when there is enlightenment, to progress towards new ventures born of new insights, conversation and risk in terms of a future. This is not only the experience of the so-called secular world, it is the experience of the theological and ecclesiastical world. Dissidence in the face of hardened and intransigent systems is an inevitability. If my junction of Inner City life, as religious and priest, has given me any insight, it is this awareness of tension between system and human experience. At the very heart of what we call Inner City, and what I would call "Innercityism", there is the ever-present tension between the amalgam of our political, social, economic and cultural systems and the human experience of the people with whom I exist.

On a level of realistic optimism, however, I believe that it is Inner City or "Innercityism" or, on a larger canvas, the powerless of this world, which offer us all an exodus to a new and nobler freedom. I no longer see, as I did once, Inner City or "Innercityism" as a mode of so-called specialised apostolates. I now see it rather as a factor, an experience, summoning the world, and therefore in a specific way, the Church, to a self-liberation, and I believe this human experience provides the basis of a "new Apologetics".

ABOUT IMPRISONMENT, ABSTRACTIONS AND ABSOLUTES

On most days of each week for close on twelve years I travelled through the scenes and places of my childhood to a place of ministry and work, a major national prison.

When I was a child the prison was a place of magnetic mystery. To see it at night was to look upon a rather macabre fairyland. It was like a large wall pinpricked with lights. The lights never appeared as lighted windows, though that is what they were. One never thought that someone had forgotten to draw the curtains or pull down the blinds, and one never thought of a light being switched on and off. It was an inhuman backdrop to the physical environment. As a child it was forbidding, threatening and, quite candidly, frightening. It was mysterious but it was magnetic. One had to look at it. I never thought in those early, carefree, childhood days that I would one day have a key to open doors behind that wall. Incidentally it is only a stone's throw from the junction platform I have spoken about.

"They" said it was a building for bad people. In fact most of "them" still say that. Have you ever reflected on the number of times in life we say: "They said ..."? One is reminded of Heidegger: "The 'they' prescribes one's state of mind and determines what and how one sees."[3] I suppose in any organised group of human beings, from the State down to the smallest club, a "they" will emerge. It emerges, I would think, basically out of the interaction of human relationships. The interaction is more often than not a power-game, no matter how open or hidden it may be, and more often than not is controlled by both a process of self-seeking and a graded commitment to a common purpose. One may hope that this struggle can be transcended and become a process of self-giving, of going out to the other, with the group held together by a mutuality of relationships and based upon an ever-evolving search for the good of the other. In such a group, justice finds its fulfilment in friendship. This is the hope we dream of and that has sometimes, throughout history, been achieved by specific gatherings of human beings: indeed, it is the Christian aspiration. But, being the human beings we are, often getting our priorities wrong, we live out our lives within a web of delicate yet uneasy social agreements. We are not all totally involved in each other's hopes, failures, achievements, joys and sorrows, and in such a situation one cannot but expect a "they" to emerge prescribing our state of mind and determining in what way we are able to perceive the world and the quest of humanity.

Whilst I could not countenance the idea that "they" define for me good and evil, it is true nevertheless that "they" shape my perception of good and evil. I need to accept this. In my own life "they" have come in many forms. My parents and teachers, the Magisterium of the Church, my friends, thinkers and doers – such are some of the constituents of my "they" and, I would think, of everyone else's. The real problem comes when a "they" begins to take hold of my life which I cannot really identify, still less have a conversation with. The point I wish to make is that our perception of right and wrong, of good and evil, is too often governed by an elusive, and sometimes illusive, "they". We can be spiritually lazy in our awareness of this reality and, falling back upon a certain self-pity or even sympathy, perhaps in a very complex world we are too weary and bewildered at times to analyse such forces. But our pyramids of power, political, social, economic and cultural are shaped, at least in part, by this "they".

The prison became for me a mirror of this social reality. Like society itself, the penal system we have today, no matter how much mature and reasoned thought has gone into it, is certainly shaped by this elusive "they". It is sometimes called "public opinion". The problem about public opinion, however, is where to locate its private beginnings. The words "good" and "evil" are used indiscriminately about prisoners. I would like to mention that my parents, in those days of my childhood when I first experienced the magnetic mysteriousness of the prison, never used such words of those "inside".

They always used the word "unfortunate". So early in my life that light pinpricked wall was about "unfortunates".

One of the characteristics of "they" is that rational argument is excluded. It is all a matter of totalities, absolutes, abstractions and the protection of the logic of the system. There is a great love of such words as "objectivity" and "neutrality". "You must look at things objectively", "they " say; "One can only be neutral and reasonable in such matters", "they" say.

I must admit to a certain suspicion of such terms. Surely, we are all caught up in the ambiguities of human existence and every statement we make is not without an emotional input? "They" avoids ambiguity.

One Christmas day in the prison I was opening one of the corridor gates for some people, from outside, who had come to sing carols. This was a regular event. As we came through the gates we had to stand back to allow a group of prisoners to walk through. One of the visitors tugged at my sleeve and in whispered tones asked me: "Would any of them be murderers or rapists?" I could understand the question and the curiosity, but both were rooted in a certain perception. When I replied that I thought not, I almost felt a certain wave of disappointment hit me. I make this point to say two things: first, that prisons are not full of rapists and murderers; second – and this is much more controversial – that in all my time in prison ministry I never came across such crimes without, at the same time, coming across unbelievably tortured minds, emotional inadequacy and tragedy-ridden backgrounds in the people concerned.

I am horrified, disgusted and saddened by child abuse, by rape, by murder, by the mugging of old people and by that whole litany of evil which makes our human pilgrimage such a sad and broken journeying. I further believe that society has a right to demand a punitive system. But it is worthwhile our remembering – taking the year 1986 as a sample – that 70 per cent of the 36,187 population sentenced and held in the prisons of England and Wales were convicted of non-violent crime.

As I have remarked, society must maintain some form of punitive system. But that punitive system must always be open to rethink and review; that punitive system must, too, always be open to the whole of society's review. Furthermore, every member of society must take responsibility for the punitive system it possesses and must face the grave responsibility of being part of an on-going dialogue about the nature and quality of that system. A prison is not some off-shore island of society; it is part and parcel of it. Indeed, the kind of punitive system any society possesses is a mirror of the nature and quality of society itself. Too often, our prisons came within the category of "dirty work for dirty hands". Too often, like the Inner City and "Innercityism", the view of the prison is shaped by the "they", out of a mediocrity of thought and a selfishness of life. I am part of that mediocrity and I am part of that selfishness. We shall be free of these only when we find different criteria to live by and different dreams to dream.

I have referred to my years of prison ministry in this meditation because they marked the major junctions in my life. Though distinct from my junction of Inner City, the prison is theologically, spiritually and politically inseparable from the Inner City, and I further believe that the prison system, a distinctive example of the logic of the system, is a mirror of the kind of philosophy, indeed even theology, which "they" would like to have at the very roots of society as a whole.

I remember one summer's day, on my way by train to fulfil a lecturing engagement in Scotland, finding myself stranded in the middle of the countryside for close on an hour. For some mechanical reason the train could not continue. Somebody remarked: "That's British Rail for you!" It was an understandable burst of impatience. But I thought to myself: "What is British Rail?" I mean, there is really no such thing as "British Rail". It is a convenient abstract entity which, to be sure, has some grounding in reality, namely, trains, managers, workers and the rest, but it does not exist except in terms of "them". And very understandably we need to use the term.

To extend the example, I often hear parents say: "We're going up to see the school." I know they don't mean the buildings; they mean, more often than not, the head-teacher or the governors. We all use such language: the State, the Party,

the Nation, the Democracy, the Religious Order, even Down-
ing Street and Buckingham Palace. We need to use such terms.
They are abstractions for living people uttering living words
and initiating living actions. The only problem is we can be
brought so to think of such abstractions as if they possessed
some kind of intrinsic mystical driving force within themselves, as distinct from the comings and goings of human
beings who give birth to the ideas which shape history. Such an
outlook or understanding of historical realities, especially
those which touch upon our own human lives in a very inti-
mate or influential manner, may awaken in us reverence which,
in its turn, prevents us from entering into life's major debates.
In fact all tyranny and all totalitarianism, no matter of what
order, invoke and encourage such an outlook of reverence. It is
an outlook which paralyses our wish to become involved. It
engenders an escapist philosophy of life which runs away from
living debate and conversation, so that phrases like "Law and
Order", "the Penal System", "Private Ownership" and so
forth are made into eternal, immortal and immutable realities
of life. They are absolutes beyond the revising or changing
force of human beings. In fact what is humanly created is, in
such a view of life, made into God.

I would not wish to be understood as advocating a totally
relative view of life. Every society needs law and order, every
society needs a punitive system, and so forth. But nothing
humanly created is beyond revision or change. The truly noble
society is forever reviewing its absolutes, making sure that they
minister to the progress and the development and the liberation of all its members. And the truly noble society is forever
vigilant about its use of abstractions.

When it comes to those other two abstractions, "Right" and
"Left" what does concern me is this: I am told that the "Right"
seems too often intent upon defining and implementing its
absolutes and abstractions, in such a way that there is a ministering to the powerful of this world at the expense of the
powerless – the debate about life's absolutes and abstractions
remains beyond the voice of the voiceless and the power of the
powerless. Certainly, in what I hear from the "Right", the

great events of history are seldom looked at from the viewpoint of those who have been marginalised, alienated and stigmatised in history. And what concerns me more, I seem to find God invoked too often as one of the absolutes which blesses the "Right" and curses the "Left". I must hasten to say that I see also an abstractionism and an absolutism on the part of the "Left", which also oppresses. It is a confusing situation.

I feel, however, that the task of the Church, the inheritance of the powerless Golgotha God, is to make sure that the great events of history are seen and understood through the eyes of the powerless, the voiceless, the marginalised, the stigmatised and the alienated. It must not allow those who wish to secure the secure and empower the powerful to hijack God as one of their absolutes and abstractions. Does this make the Church "Left"? Many seem to think so. We have seen how very mild statements made by bishops, priests, religious, Christian men and women, on behalf of the powerless in our society have been portrayed as seedlings of revolution. One cannot but wonder what the reaction would be were we really to preach the totality of the Gospel from the viewpoint of the marginalised and the powerless. Certainly the voice of the "they" would thunder in the land louder than any of the Old Testament prophets. But, then, one of the problems of the "they", theologically, has always been an acceptance of a generic condemnation of idolatry but a profound rejection of anyone who would name the idols.

Am I now suggesting that the "they" is the "Right"? In the light of my earlier remarks concerning who does and who does not view life through the eyes of the powerless and the marginalised, I have to say that such is my suggestion. And it is this "they" which would, *mutatis mutandis*, feel comfortable with a society not unlike what I found and ministered to in the prison. It would be a society able to retire each night without too much anxiety about the phenomenon of "Innercityism".

CHAPTER SEVEN

Pyramids of Power and Powerlessness

The "They" I have spoken about is not self-creative: it is the consequence of a dialogue, a dialectic, even a struggle, which is the very dynamism of what we call "society". Society is a vague term denoting essentially a web of social relationships and, for the most part, agreed aims and objectives. What questions and answers create the dialogue, the dialectic or, even the struggle, at the heart of society is obviously open to dispute. But if I am attempting to live a meaningful life I cannot avoid being part of a "conversation" centred upon four major questions:

1 How are the material resources of this world to be organised?
2 How is power over our destiny to be organised and defined?
3 How are my social relationships to be organised and defined?
4 How are they defined and who defines, the ideas which shape my life and my action?

Each of these questions implies both the possession and exercise of power, power within the economic, political, social and cultural or ideological systems which create the major parameters of personal and social life. But not only am I caught up in a conversation created by these questions and the answers given; the answers given also create the structures and institutions in which I live and participate. It is a matter of justice that each member of society should be able to live in and participate in this conversation of the institutions and structures with freedom, equality and fullness of human life.

The reason these ideals are not currently realised in society, is that the structures and the institutions exist in the mode of a pyramid. There is an apex, a middle and a base. The lower one is down that pyramid the less one is able to participate in the on-going conversation of life. One moves from powerful elitism at the apex, in each pyramid, to powerless dependency at the base. I belong, as priest and religious, to that middle sector of the pyramid; I belong to those people

> who are not very wealthy or powerful themselves, but the work they do maintains the power of those at the top of the pyramid. The organisations which they staff have a double purpose. On the one hand they are normally there to meet a real need of the community – for example, the health services, security, information, food, etc – but they also have a second purpose, which is less obvious: to promote the interests of those who exercise control and ensure that they do not lose their power.[1]

This pattern of power belongs to the whole world.

I often reflected, as I walked around prison landings and corridors, how dependent we all were upon the passive benevolence of the prisoner. That may seem a rather strange remark, but there were, at certain times in my ministry in the prison, close on 1,500 prisoners. The environment was not so much punitive as dehumanising. I do not mean that every officer, or for that matter the prison hierarchy, necessarily went out of their way to dehumanise the prisoner; I had, and still have, many friends in the prison service whom I admire, and they were not men committed to a project of dehumanisation – on the contrary, many attempted to understand and help prisoners. But the environment, to put it mildly, was not one which contributed to human development. Lack of toilets, systems of communication based upon the barked order and such factors did not contribute to the best of "being human". If the actual prisoner population had decided, through organised leadership, to rebel against this, we should have had very little chance of winning, but the prison population, for the most part, out of self-interest or sheer apathy, went along with the logic of the system, and order was maintained. I called this "going-along-with" passive benevolence. In other words, everyone for the most part agreed to "stay in their place". This is what "the 'They'" depends upon. The pyramid will not collapse as long as everyone stays in his place. The prison, like so many institutions and structures in society, depended upon this. As long as the situation remains such, nobody need really reflect or think: the task is simply to keep the pyramid standing firm and erect.

In fact and in effect, the prison symbolised for me a perfect model of the society "They" want and wish and strive to keep alive and well. I used to think even God was fitted into this society. He had virtually taken the Official Secrets Act. He was made part of it. Denominationally, God was a red card for Roman Catholics, blue for Jews and white for everyone else. The chaplaincy, and all other "caring" services, wandered up and down the pyramid dispensing care and compassion. The chaplaincy specifically attempted to minister God. There could be law as long as this order was part of the logic of the system. To disturb the logic of the system was not without its dangers and inconveniences. One could permutate the applications of the law but one could not, perhaps dared not, question the understanding of order. As long as this situation continued, the world at large could sleep in peace. The prison, as I have suggested, was an off-shore island. There was a base, a middle and an apex to the prison pyramid. One should not be surprised at this because there is a base, a middle and an apex to all society's pyramids. Such pyramids may be disturbed by physical violence, admittedly, but, at all costs, one does not disturb such a situation with conversation, exchange of ideas, communicate with the base in a constructive manner or reflect upon the questions of why is there a base and where did the base come from and should there be a base. To do so means all sectors of the pyramid are called into accountability and, indeed, may have to rethink radically their ideas about life. I believe, however, such questioning is an essential part of the Church's mission.

Am I, then, calling into question or denying the need for law and order, for certain systems of control, for the communal and personal acceptance of responsibilities? Of course not, but I am suggesting that none of these realities is beyond revision, beyond reshaping or questioning. To recall a theme already spoken about, whilst society needs certain absolutes to live by and through, since such absolutes are humanly created, they can be reshaped, and certain expressions of such absolutes, when they are seen to be no longer authentically contributing to the general common good, must be allowed to die.

As a priest and religious I have come to believe that Christianity, in general, and the institutional Church, in particular, are called to challenge the "They" from the perspective of the most powerless in this world. In this context the Church – I will remain with that term – must identify its role as teacher and its role as agitator, for I believe it must be both. I am not suggesting that Jesus was an agitator or a revolutionary in our contemporary political sense, so I would not wish to define the mission of Jesus in political, economic, social or cultural terms. But he did seek power: it was the power of a redefined love. And despite all the necessary qualifications, one cannot but think twice when one reads about such alliances as the one spoken of in Mark's Gospel: "The Pharisees went out, and immediately held counsel with the Herodians against him, how to destroy him."[2] In a word, Jesus was perceived as a disturbance at the base of the pyramid.

> And they would have liked to arrest him, because they realised that the parable [of the Wicked Husbandmen] was aimed at them, but they were afraid of the crowds.... It was two days before the Passover and the feast of Unleavened Bread, and the chief priests and the scribes were looking for a way to arrest Jesus by some trick and have him put to death. For they said, "It must not be during the festivities, or there will be a disturbance among the people...."[3]

The people were obviously not the priests and scribes, they

were not the Romans, they were not the Sadducees – the people were the marginalised, the alienated, the stigmatised, the powerless. Jesus was not executed on the grounds of mistaken identity or misunderstanding. The mission of redefined love, with a vision of a new reign of God, had serious social consequences. Jesus knew the implications of his message and refused to be distracted from that journey to Jerusalem of which we have already spoken.

> They reached Jerusalem and he went into the Temple and began driving out those who were selling and buying there; he upset the tables of the money changers ... "does not scripture say: 'My house will be called a house of prayer for all the peoples?' But you have turned it into a robber's den." This came to the ears of the chief priests and the scribes, and they tried to find some way of doing away with him; they were afraid of him because the people were carried away by his teaching.[4]

As we struggle to prove and affirm Jesus's resurrection, we must also understand and live by his choice of the powerless and his confrontation with those who would oppress them, simultaneously claiming Yahweh as the ultimate affirmation and approbation of their own definition and exercise of power.

I am not, of course, suggesting that Jesus discussed with his disciples the distribution of economic resources, the exercise of political power, the development of the social relationships of his time or the problems of contemporary ideological influences, in the language and thought patterns of our times. But I am convinced that paradigms of power, which pushed people into the margins of life and constructed life-styles which denied the "little ones" of this world authentic participation in planning their own lives, were a concern of the one we perceive and believe to be the word of God who called all human beings into a creative partnership in this world. Therefore it is impossible to have *a religious thing* totally apart from *a political thing*. An attempt to understand the religious reality demands coming to grips with the political reality. Certain political, economic, social and cultural developments in our own times are not merely unjust, they are also blasphemous.

One morning in the prison will always be with me to my dying day. The memory of it is rooted in what was an almost casual conversation. One prisoner, Tom, who had become a good friend of mine over the years asked me had I ever needed God. I did not think it was the time for, or for that matter that the question demanded, neat theological distinctions between the necessity and contingency of human existence. Had I ever needed God? Before I could even begin to struggle with the answer a further qualification was added. "Have you ever needed God because there was nowhere else to go?" Such was the final version of Tom's question. The question was then given its personal gloss. "When you're an alcoholic and you've lost everything, you go to sleep on the park bench, you wake up having wet yourself and kids dance around you – then there's only God, there's nowhere to go." I knew his background, I knew what had sparked it all off years ago. There was nowhere to go. Of course, he needed help, but that kind of predictable commonsense, middle-of-the-pyramid advice, really offered nothing. I said to him, from the depths of my own honesty: "Tom, I've never in my life had nowhere to go."

As I made my way back to the Inner City from the prison, through the scenes of my childhood, I thought to myself, "I am driving home through one example of my 'somewhere to go'. I am driving home through God." I was visiting the points of my "Clock of Influence", points which had been mediation Godly moments. I was going through examples of my life's junctions. They symbolise love and welcome, joy and happiness, memories of a warm hearth in spite of poverty in days gone by – this is all my God. This is how, in the concrete, God had been mediated to me in life. To be sure, in later life there had been moments of darkness, moments of terrible aloneness, moments of seemingly insoluble doubt. But I have to admit, even in the depths of darkness of whatever kind, there had always been somewhere to go. If, even without my conscious realisation, God had been given to me, God had never ceased to be made flesh. The word made flesh had always called to me in human words, addressed my soul, drawn me into a loving and liberating conversation, because of all the human words calling out to me, addressing my spirit, drawing me into loving and liberating conversations. What is God? Where is God? Surely in this burst of human acts and words, alive with kindness and understanding, with correction and rebuke, with a loving series of friendships, when I experienced a unity of spirit with other human beings! This is the God of history, ever ancient and ever new. Paradoxically, there can be no divine without the human and there can be no human without the divine.

Whatever the correct exegesis may be, God has given us a "nowhere-to-go-God" by giving us an abandoned God. This is to be found in those Golgotha words, which isolate God from God. "My God, my God, why have you forsaken me?" Did this Jesus have nowhere to go at one point in life, except into the depths of a seemingly absurd and quixotic death? Yet even at that point of desolation there were a few friends at his place of execution. He still had somewhere to go. Does God, the eternal artist, paint a picture for us of the horror of a nowhere-to-go experience? It is surely not a romanticisation of such a predicament. It is rather a portent of all our gas chambers, of our besieged townships, of the bases of all our pyramids of power, in a word, of all our horrific acts of dehumanisation.

The Christian mystics do not turn God into a human lover, friend, brother or sister, speaking in a recognisable human language, because they wish to make God recognisable to humanity. God made sure of that. They could not do otherwise. I cannot get to God unless I turn God into my human patterns of thought and speech. God has recognised this in the Christian vision of life by actually agreeing to be part of that human condition. For the true Christian, dehumanisation is dedivinisation and dedivinisation is dehumanisation. This is the process in which we are summoned to discover both ourselves and God. It is not a question of *our* not being able to do it any other way; God could not do it any other way.

Words like "social teaching" or "social doctrine" or even "social Gospel", are very dangerous. They can give the impression that the discovery of the political, economic, social and cultural in Gospel or Church terms is the discovery of a separate reality – separate, that is, from the so-called "spiritual" message of the Gospel. But one cannot have that Gospel without this social reality, because the social reality is the logical consequence of the integral Gospel. If it causes ambiguity, so be it. All I need do is recognise the fact that there is no mediation of God, a mediation concretised in the human acts and movements of history, which is not touched with the ambiguous and the problematic. There is no packaged God. I must seek union with God through a union with my brothers and sisters in this world because God is seeking union with me through my brothers and sisters. This is the only real road for me in life. I cannot escape it. And if I accept this I cannot escape the systems, structures and institutions which are the fruits of human commitment. I cannot be at ease, I cannot rest, if the world in which I live leaves even one brother or sister with nowhere to go. In my world I must face up to the fact, no matter how frustrating and disturbing the fact may be that too many of our systems, structures and institutions, along with the philosophies and theologies which underpin them, carry the sinfulness and self-seeking of a weak and self-destructive humanity. If I believe my Christian vision is meant to influence and leaven my life's judgements, then there is nothing on earth which can escape that influence. There are no "neutral" issues or events.

Gilson once remarked that there was nothing pious in being wrong about God. The context of his reflection was a calling into question those systems of spirituality, no matter how well intentioned, which call for a "simple faith" at all times, avoiding the paths of questioning and reflection.[5]

There is wisdom in Gilson's remark. And there is wisdom too in the counsels of the author of the *Imitation of Christ*.

> It is certain that learned speeches do not make a man holy and just; it is a virtuous life that makes him dear to God. I would rather feel sorrow for my sins than be able to define it. If you know the whole Bible by heart, and all that the philosophers have said, what use would it all be to you without the love of God and grace?[6]

But the crucial questions, I would think, are at a different level.

How and when do I know I am right about God? How and when do I know God's love and grace is with me?

There are times in life when, contemplating a world of pain and suffering, even the most convinced believer wonders about the "tremendous silence" of this all-loving God. When the Church says God is in that silence or that I must respond with a simplicity of belief at such junctions of doubt, it may well offer a temporary path, but that does not make sense to me or, even more so, to an unbelieving and puzzled world.

I need to confess that the God who dominates my life at this stage of my life is not without connections with the God of my childhood. It was the God given me at the family fireside. Indeed, there is truth in the fact that God captured my soul by a gift called "faith", but that too was mediated to me. On the other hand, I have certainly been drawn more and more into a search for where, how and when, I am to recognise God. At the heart of that search has been a question about God in making sense of this process that we call human life and action.

I remember reading one night, the day's work finished, these moving and disturbing words of the Argentinian poet, Atahulpa Yupanqui:

One day I asked my Grandfather:
"Grandfather, where is God?"
He looked at me sadly
But never said a word.
My grandfather died in the fields
Without a priest or doctor;
And the Indians buried him
Playing bamboo flutes and drums.

Later I asked my father:
"Father, what do you know of God?"
My father became very serious
But never said a word.
My father died in the mines
Without a priest or doctor;
And the Indians buried him
Playing bamboo flutes and drums.

My brother lives in the hills

And he never sees a flower;
Only sweat, malaria and snakes
And the life of the woodcutter.
Let no one ask him
If he knows where God is!
Such an important gentleman
Has not passed near his house!

I sing along the roads
And when I am in prison
I hear the voices of the people
Who sing better than I,
Saying that God cares for the poor.
Well that may be true or not.
But I know for a fact
That he dines with the mine-owner.

There is something on earth
That is more important than God
That no one should spit blood
Just to let others live better.[7]

I would hope, indeed struggle for, an understanding of a God who will not be where some "spit blood, just to let others live better". Is this being wrong about God? Is this a failure to understand the mysterious love and grace of God?

There is no human word, there is no human action, which can carry the fullness of God or express the fullness of God. Whatever I say and whatever I do, because of what I am, a finite and contingent being, can never captivate God. There are moments in all our lives which seem to touch a joy beyond expression; there are moments of peace which are beyond our human words. And there are actions in human life which, as it has been said before, constitute a "rumour" about God. They go out beyond the space and time which, too often, lie heavy upon us; the space and time which seem to imprison our human spirits. All such words or actions or moments which create the world in which we dwell and seek to develop are words of God. And there are words and actions which create ideologies and systems and structures in which I find no sign of God. If God is fitted into them, then those who so shape God must be called to account. Of course, we all carry the blame, we are all marked with such sinfulness. At the end of the twentieth century, however, searching for God and understanding God in such a way is, I believe, fundamental to any "new Apologetics".

I believe that, in the divided world in which we find ourselves, dwelling in the midst of our destructive paradigms of power and powerlessness, such a search will lead us to a piety that is based upon a rightness about God and will help to deliver to the love of God a world graced in a justice fulfilled in love.

For Jesus there were words only about the rule or Kingdom of God; there was so little about the Godhead. It is like a man or woman who begins to tell you about the wonder of a friend, but can only ultimately describe moments of friendship. So I find myself searching now more often than not for signs of the Kingdom, seldom for a God. Yet I know in that Kingdom I must and will find God. Where is justice? Where is truth? Where is love? Where is the peacemaker? Where is compassion? Such questions must lead me to where God is. *Ubi caritas, ibi Deus.* And if I am so led to God through these marks of the Kingdom, a kingdom sometimes without explicitness, then I must be led, too, along a road of confrontation face to face with systems, structures and ideologies which fail to honour such qualities. God is not competitive; God does not bless privilege; God does not bless ownership of the things of this world simply for the sake of ownership; God does not marginalise the weak of this world; God does not distinguish between the races; God does not romanticise human suffering; God's starting point is with the powerless. If to have such a vision of God and to believe that such a vision is to be implemented is a dream, so be it. Dream though it may be, it is certainly not the living nightmare with which we are called to live, too often, in our contemporary world. The nightmare is so frightening and horrific because God appears to bless and consecrate our injustices. Such a part God cannot, will not accept, in the drama of time and eternity. Jesus knew this.

Bring me your worthless offerings no more...
I cannot endure festival and solemnity...
You may multiply your prayers, I shall not listen.
Your hands are covered with blood, wash, make yourselves clean.
Take your wrong-doing out of my sight.
Cease to do evil.
Learn to do good,
Search for justice,
help the oppressed,
be just to the orphan
plead for the widow.[8]

I hate and despise your feasts,
I take no pleasure in your solemn festivals.
When you offer me holocausts,
I reject your oblations...
Let me have no more of the din of your chanting, no more of your
    strumming on harps.
But let justice flow like water and integrity like an unfailing
    stream.[9]

Fasting like yours today will never make your voice heard on high.
Is that the sort of fast that pleases me, a truly penitential day for
    men?
Hanging your head like a reed, lying down on sackcloth and ashes?
Is that what you call fasting, a day acceptable to Yahweh?
Is not this the sort of fast that pleases me – it is the Lord Yahweh
    who speaks – to break unjust fetters and undo the thongs of the
    yoke,
to let the oppressed go free,
and break every yoke,
to share your bread with the hungry,
and shelter the homeless poor,
to clothe the man you see to be naked
and not turn from your kin?
Then will your light shine like the dawn and your wound be
    quickly healed over
Your integrity will go before you and the glory of Yahweh behind
    you.
Cry, and Yahweh will answer;
call, and he will say, "I am here".[10]

When Jesus spoke about offering a gift at the altar, then as we
suddenly remember the breakdown in relationships with

others, about our having to leave the gift and seek reconcilia-
tion first, he was speaking the new commandment of love and
offering a dream, a dream built upon his own understanding of
the prophets. If I cannot live up to that dream, then at least I
must feel a deep sense of unease. My inclination has been, too
often, to translate the dream into personal meaning and language. And I have also, too often, backed my interpretation
with a politics of commonsense and reasonableness, but I now
realise how short this falls.

It is not so much that I must find a new way to integrate into
my Christian life and vision this reality of the social and the
political. It is, rather that my Christian life and vision depend
upon a distinctive understanding and interpretation of the
social and the political experience. Indeed, this is what has been
for me, in a very special way, the significance of my Inner City
junction. In other words, I have not found a new work to do; I
find myself faced with a new theological and spiritual source. I
would not wish to give the impression that this suddenly
happened to me when I arrived in the Inner City. But the Inner
City has become, so to speak, the clinching argument. In other
words, I was faced more with the question of the quality and
nature of existence, rather than the quality and nature of
action.

I do stand, in a sense, in a total aloneness before God, as we
all do if we believe in God. I look into a life that is marked by
personal selfishness, personal self-seeking and spiritual failure.
There is a sense – in an old spiritual language, and still not
without use – I feel my own "nothingness'. Indeed, too often,
in life I have chosen a certain "nothingness". Having said that,
however, there is another dimension: it is the prepositional
dimension of "with".

The preposition has cosmological and psychological consequences. "I exist *with*", not only a God I attempt to describe
and understand, but also a world I must make sense of to recall
the words of Sartre, with which I began this meditation. Unlike
with Sartre, God has been an important, indeed a vital, ingredient in my life. God has been so, for through the word God,
through the langauge of "*Godness*", I have attempted to recog-

nise, or better I attempt now to recognise, the ultimately undefinable quality of the other human being. I attempt to touch the spirit of the other; I am brought into the sanctuary of the spirit of the other or the transcendence of the other. To be sure, many of my brothers and sisters believe they can do this without an understanding of God or the use of "God language". I am only attempting to define or describe what the word God has come to mean in my life. It leads me, in the words of Berdyaev, to that

> communion in sympathy and love, and the overcoming of estrangement; personalism and the expression of the individual and personal character of each existence; a transition to the realm of freedom and the determination from within, with victory over enslaving necessity; and the predominance of quality over quantity, of creativeness over adaptation.[11]

Above all things I feel that an understanding of God has led me to a deepening of an understanding of existing with, suffering with and acting with other human beings. It is a "withness" which truly hears the cry, the appeal, the hope and the despair of "the others" through "the Other", who knew our experience in one other known as Jesus.

I have heard the cry of the others who struggle to utter the words "I am" in the midst of a world, which politically, socially, economically and culturally, implicitly at least, says "You are not." Thus there is a divide opened between the name of God and the name of some of those, the marginalised, the stigmatised, the alienated and the powerless, who are equally made in the likeness and image of God and, therefore, possess an inalienable right to invoke God's name and exercise their creative existence. A Church institutionally cannot utter the vision of that "I am", which is God, and in which we all participate, unless its symbolism of life, word, action and structure give credibility to its utterance. Let us stay awhile with this name of God, "I am who am", for in its mystery is to be found not only our wonder and glory, but also the clue to our understanding and critique of our pyramids of power and powerlessness. Indeed, it is this mysterious name which under-pins much of the contemporary violence which signals the collapse of the pyramid.

> Then Moses said to God ... "But if they ask me what his name is, what am I to tell them?" And God said to Moses, "I Am who I Am. This," he added "is what you must say to the sons of Israel: 'I Am has sent me to you'."[12]

Fundamental to any understanding of the Judaeo-Christian tradition is the understanding of the Exodus, the delivery from oppression. In the history of Moses and the liberation of Abraham's descendants from Egypt we see the most dramatic symbols of the Jewish experience of God in history. Christianity specifically took up the same theme in terms of the death and resurrection of Jesus; to pass over from bondage to freedom is a radical theme of the authentic Judaeo-Christian tradition. If that tradition either fails to proclaim this or, worse still, from an elitist perspective oppresses others, the tradition is corrupted. But we must be very careful not to spiritualise the Exodus. The cry, "Let my people go!", must have resonance in the total human being, in the flesh and the spirit, uniquely one, of every man and woman and child. Too often, I believe, both Jew and Christian, though persecuted historically and put into bondage, have been careless with the wholeness of this tradition.

I like to believe that the key to this understanding of whole-ness is to be located in God's honouring the glory and the wonder of the unqualified act of existence, being and living. There can be no exodus from bondage to freedom, no passing over from imprisonment to liberty, which fails to honour that wholeness of humanity and fails to see that wholeness rooted in the simple words, "I am". It has been said, and so truly, that

> I am is the unqualified fullness of being,
> is the supreme indication of presence,
> is the one statement that cannot be uttered without being com-pletely true,
> is the one completely and immediately personal statement,

is presupposed in every intelligible utterance,
is true equally of God and Man,
is true in every time and place,
is the name of God.

When Moses was given the task of leadership in the movement of liberation, the God who sent him uttered a name, "I
Am who I Am". The statement leads us to the threshold of
supernatural mystery about the nature of God, at which threshold I utter, "I believe"; it also leads us to the frontiers of a
natural mystery about the very nature of the human being, at
which threshold the nature of my Credo may be different, but
still I must honour with a delicate respect and reverence the
unique human being. I am hard put to find a definition of the
human being and I am forced into vast descriptions to communicate the wonder of humanity. The human being defies
human language: it is almost impossible to "get at" the very
essence of a human being. I am forced into wonder, awe and
contemplation. This is not to suggest that I am forced into a
world of irrationality; it is simply to say that this rich and
wonderful complexity I call humanity so often escapes my
language of rational discourse. The human being only corrupts
itself, turns in upon itself to its own destruction, when it fails to
honour the multiplicities of its own expression. That is to say it
corrupts itself when one human being, or a class of human
beings, fails to understand or so acts against other human
beings who participate in the glory of the words, "I am". That
is the point at which a vision of unique personalism surrenders
to an oppressive individualism.

My "I am" participates in the "I am" of God. My "I am"
must, above all things, be able to reach a fullness in the creative
"I am" of God. And as the "I am" of God rejects an individualism by the very fact of a "going out" to the world in a creative
act, so each human "I am" can only build a bridge to God,
truly worship God, and reflect back to God the image in which
it is made, by going out in creative acts to the world that is
around it. When structures and ideologies fail to realise this
name of God and its human consequences, even if they fail or

reject the believing vision which I hold to, they are doomed to destruction – which can be ours as well, because they become the cause of violence. In other words, all philosophies, regimes, ideologies, institutions and structures will finally collapse if they fail to recognise the uniqueness of what it is to be a true human being. For this reason, the difference between my "I am" and the "I am" of God rests in my necessary dependencies face to face with the utter independence of God. Thus I am dependent upon many realities and philosophies at work in this world to realise the fullness of my "I am". The "I am" of history has been, and will continue to be, the final argument against "the They".

A true understanding of this name of God, at this stage of my life, becomes for me the root of all my believing. It leads me to an understanding of the totality of Jesus's mission. It leads me to the understanding of the God who is

> the incomprehensible goal of human transcendence. This God communicates himself to man existentially as a forgiving and as a fulfilling love which we call grace ... [to] Man [who] fulfils himself only if he gives himself away radically to his neighbour. In this dangerous venture ... man grasps at least implicitly the meaning of God as the horizon and guarantee of radical love. For God in his self-communication alone provides the possibility and the ground of such a love. This love is individually intimate as well as social, and the basic unity of these two qualities gives a real foundation to the Church. [Thus] Christianity keeps open the question of the "Absolute Future". This absolute future can only be given in the self-communication of God. God's will to communicate himself is irrevocably ratified in Jesus Christ.[13]

But there can be no understanding, communication or appreciation of an "Absolute Future" without a relative future. That is to say, human beings must be able to see a future and, indeed, invest in a future in this world. Whilst in Christian terms one is caught up in a "not yet" related to the whole of history, I must not create or participate in the creation of any "not yet" in history which blesses or spiritualises ideologies and institutions which marginalise and oppress the powerless. Indeed, I must not even agree to co-exist with them, never mind bless or spiritualise them. On the contrary, I must confront them. Not to do so is to blaspheme the name of God and the name of humanity by a process of manipulative escapism in the name of my own comfort. This, I believe, is at the heart of the mystery of the dead Golgotha God and the risen Galilean God. "I Am who I Am" died in horrific suffering and rose in wondrous glory to liberate, personally and communally, each and every "I am" of history. "I am" of history must be able to live out a total hopefulness in the light of both an "Absolute Future" and a "Relative Future". This leads me to accept, from another context, the words of Péguy:

> Everything begins in mysticism and ends in politics. The interest, the question, the essential is that in each other, in each system, mysticism be not devoured by the politics of which it gave birth. Politics laugh at mysticism, but it is still mysticism which feeds these same politics.[14]

The mystical name of God spills over into the name of humanity and makes humanity itself deserving of an honour which is rooted in the mystical.

Theology is faith seeking understanding. And I affirm and remain conscious of the necessary distinction between faith and reason, between the natural and the supernatural; but, whilst making sure that faith is not swallowed up by reason or reason is destroyed by faith, a totality of life in wonderful unity becomes vital in my life for the Christian community. It was Leibniz, in the *Confessio Philosophi*, who put the words into the mouth of the theologian addressing the philosopher: "*Laudo modestiam tuam ... Instrumentum in te habebo* (I praise your modesty ... In you I will have an instrument."[15]

But, buried both in the search of the philosopher and in the very subject the philosopher pursues, signs of God's wonder are to be found, so modesty must not be confused with an apology for existence. And though my faith may lead me to address the world as but a reflection of God's wonder, it remains still the result of God's creative act. The wonder and the reflection must be truly honoured, and I must be ready to join hands with all those who seek to develop and liberate that world, no matter how we may differ in matters of faith. If I seek to honour God without a profound care for the world in which I live, that carelessness with the world is a carelessness with God. Thus in my life there is always at work a dialectic. I cannot escape, if I truly love both God and the world, the quest, sometimes not without suffering, for a living synthesis. Jesus gave notice of the peril involved in such escapism.

> It is not those who say to me, "Lord, Lord," who will enter the Kingdom of Heaven, but the person who does the will of my Father in Heaven.[16]

That will concerns surely the care of God's creation and God's creatures. The synthesis was made very clear in the Judgement scene, where Jesus is seen in the hungry, the thirsty, the stranger, the naked, the sick and the imprisoned. But that synthesis of reaching for and solidarity with the powerless will take a different form in every age, so that the mode of my ministering must change accordingly. As virtue is embodied in living human beings and our ideologies and institutions, so will sinfulness likewise appear. Sinfulness, like virtue, is to be found not only in the secrecy of my life but also in my actions and the consequences of my actions. No more profound sinfulness can there be than that which props up power structures that oppresses the powerless. And the greatest scandal of all is to build a self-serving scaffolding around the collapsing pyramids of power in an age when a new Magnificat is to be heard at the base, demanding recognition and liberation of the powerless. This cry and struggle of the powerless is a distinctive articulation of God's name, "I Am who I Am" echoed in their suffering, a suffering which reduces the "I am" to the form "I wish to be".

CHAPTER EIGHT

Signs of the Times

When I was a student to the priesthood, and through to the years of my being a young priest, the word "laity" became a dominant concept in my life. To a large extent, this word came to me not only from my reading, but from my familiarity with two Catholic movements which had a profound influence upon my life, the Young Christian Workers and the Young Christian Students. I believe, however, that my interest had deeper roots put down in my childhood. My father was devoted to the St Vincent de Paul Society. I remember Christmas time vividly – our "front parlour", as we called it, was full of parcels to be given to the poor, even though we as a family had precious little ourselves. I should add that the "charity" orientation, especially in my father, was kept in proportion by a strong political critique but I was always conscious of the fact that my father helped the priests and did work in the parish.

The word "laity", then, of later years, was a sophisticated form rooted in experience. Thus God, recalling the very first thoughts in my meditation, was mediated very early, beyond dogmatic and catechetical concepts and language, through a living experience growing out of my family's association with the parish.

Outdoor preaching for the Catholic Evidence Guild, the Young Christian Students, the Young Christian Workers, the Catholic Social Guild and the Legion of Mary, to mention but a few movements which became part and parcel of my life, always kept alive in me this idea of experience of the "laity", as opposed to the "priesthood", a distinction which remained until much later in life, vital in my theology.

One would hardly call the Angelicum University at Rome a

hotbed of revolution and radicalism, especially in 1954, yet it was there in the 1950s, as I read not theology but philosophy, that my mind came under new influences – it was a major junction of my life. This was before I became actively engaged in the movements I have mentioned. Having experienced them, however, theoretically, and when I returned to them from Rome, practically, my mind had changed. The distinction of priesthood and laity was still uppermost in my mind, but questions began to emerge. They were not questions about the reality of priesthood and laity, but they were questions about their nature and relationship. No matter how vaguely, I began to ask questions of myself and, implicitly, of the institutional Church. It is curious, when I look back, but the very life I was living, namely, the religious life, never featured high on the agenda of my questioning. Thus my priesthood was more dominant a reality than my religious life. For some years, too, certainly since 1948, I had been acutely aware of the Worker Priest movement in France.

When, thirty-one years ago, on 25 January 1959, at St Paul's Outside the Walls, Pope John XXIII first made it known to the world that he intended to call a Council, the first question in my mind was about the "world" and the "laity'. I believe many of my generation had the same thought. Thirty years on I have to say that not very much has happened. I seem to have lived through an era of meetings and councils, the latter on a more minor level, involved in a "tired agenda'. This is not to suggest that Vatican II (as we call it), which lasted from October 1962 to December 1965, achieved nothing. Far from it – but I do feel that results have not lived up to expectations. Nevertheless, Vatican II was a turning point, a major junction, in all our Christian lives, addressing itself as it did to the radical question: "How do we initiate and carry through a conversation with the world?" Or put another way: 'How are we to set an agenda, for the next century, which will energise Christianity as it addresses the major questions of our time?"

Throughout the post-Conciliar years this was the question which kept on surfacing. It simmered in all the General Chapter meetings, in all the newly-formed Councils of Laity and Clergy, in the subsequent synods and, too, in my own journeyings to various religious groupings both in Italy, the United Kingdom and in the United States.

No matter what my reflections may now be upon that event, it was a crucial and radical junction in the Christian pilgrimage. I have to say now, in the evening of my own life, and not without a measure of regret, that we were too concerned with what would live rather than what must die. This is not without some connection with an understanding of the Golgotha God. Was there too much about the Resurrection and not enough about the Death of Jesus? I don't know. Suffice it to say that much was achieved, but a long road seems to stretch in front of us and we must still walk it. I sometimes feel we failed to hear the cry of humanity to save it from itself. To be sure, we wrote our documents – and wonderful documents they are – but documents need translation into human life, need always to be modified by human life, and too often their words died on the winds of the world's change. Stability is never realised unless it can cope with the questionings of change. Being must always respect becoming, hierarchy must always take seriously community, dialogue must work peacefully with dialectic, experiment must always bow to pioneering and conversation must remain conscious of its own potential decay without creativity and the risk forever present to creativity. The fact is that "world" and "laity" loomed large and demanded an examination of, not to say a revolution in, the Christian understanding of power. Books like Congar's *Laypeople in the Church*[1] became handbooks for the more committed and the "world" had taken to itself a distinctive meaning, very different from the theology and spirituality of the past. The Church could never be the same again.

Vatican II was one of those great and creative moments of history, its summoning made one feel good to be alive. The event itself cannot be separated from the man responsible for it.

John XXIII openly renounced the nostalgic yearnings for a Christendom on the medieval pattern in which concord between nations was the result of their common obedience to impulses from the

Vatican. Inspired by his optimistic view of the potentialities of human nature, John XXIII did not hesitate to make central to his message a theme that under Pius XII was only muted, the necessity for all members of the great human family to work together to make this world a better place.[2]

Always faithful to the logic of the system, John XXIII was profoundly sensitive to the logic of experience as well. He was radically concerned about a quest for the mediation, and the meaning and manner of the mediation, of God in *our* world. The motivation behind his own commitment was a

> fundamental vision: that of achieving, even at the present time, despite divisions and opposing viewpoints, the beginnings of a unanimity between all men of good will, on the basis of a common denominator acceptable to believers and unbelievers alike. John XXIII argued that, instead of continually harping on all the ways in which the Church's positions differed from those of others, the Church should start by explaining in simple, human and comradely language those parts of her message that coincided with what he once described as "the primordial inheritance of all mankind".[3]

"The primordial inheritance of all mankind"; what does such a phrase mean? Perhaps I hold to too optimistic a view of human nature, but I do believe that there is in us all an urge, perhaps even an *élan vital*, to use Bergson's phrase, to be creative in matters of love, peace and justice. To be sure, there is also that constant inability to get our priorities right. We are weak and imperfect beings, personally and communally. And though too often we are destructively violent, cosmologically and psychologically, we are capable of great moments of creativity. I believe this to be "the primordial inheritance of all mankind". It would emerge more frequently, and indeed more powerfully, if only we talked more often with each other more openly and sensitively. In authentic conversation is to be found personal and communal liberation. In a word, authentic conversation determines both our possession and exercise of power.

I can almost hear the expressions of horror. What, more talk? Well, there's talk and there's talk. There's talk which has built into it both listening and hearing; and there's talk which is nothing but listening. And there's talk without answering or exchange of ideas whatsoever. Authentic conversation liberates human beings, it delivers up one human spirit to another in a process of mutual exchange of ideas. By this I do not suggest that conversation automatically creates reform, renewal or, indeed, revolutions in ideologies and structures; but such transference of power must begin in conversation. Indeed, those who wish to stamp out a process of radical change must silence all exchange of ideas. Aristotle reflected on this:

> There are two quite different methods, or rather principles of method, by which tyrannies can be made to last. I deal first with what may be called the traditional method, since it has been the administrative principle followed by most tyrants. Periander of Corinth is credited with having introduced many of the ways of applying it, but the Persian government offers many parallels. Here belong all the old hints for the preservation (save the mark!) of tyranny, such as, "Cut off the tops and get rid of men of independent views" and "Don't allow getting together in clubs for social and cultural activities or anything of that kind; these are the breeding grounds of independence and self-confidence, two things which a tyrant must guard against", and "Don't allow schools or other institutions where men pursue learning together, and generally ensure that people do not get to know each other well, for that establishes mutual confidence."[4]

I so reflect for two major reasons. One concerns the unique contribution of the institutional Church as symbolised in John XXIII's project. Secondly, such a reflection helps me to bring my meditation into that vital junction of my own religious life and priesthood, the Inner City. Concerning the former, Peter Hebblethwaite has written:

> John's originality can be put this way. Whereas in the nineteenth century the Church defended its own institutional rights against a state perceived to be hostile, *Pacem in Terris* gives the priority to the rights of individual human persons, whoever they may be. It therefore speaks up on behalf of minorities ... and refugees ... Again, while the nineteenth century was suspicious of the language of "human rights" as the slogan of the French Revolution,

John saw human rights as fundamental to the preaching of the Gospel. For the act of faith is free. And while the nineteenth century *magisterium* thought Catholicism should unashamedly use the state to maintain its dominance where it could, John envisaged a pluralist society in which Church and State are distinct, and therefore could be well disposed towards each other. But to start from the dignity of the human person was not to introduce a new element into "Catholic social doctrine"; the novelty lay in the way it was applied.[5]

Returning to my earlier terminology, I believe, John XXIII wanted an authentic conversation with humanity, which conversation would profoundly honour "the primordial inheritance of all mankind". The key to this desire I perceive in a certain phrase found both in the document by which John convoked the Council and in the encyclical he offered the world, *Pacem in Terris*, during the Council itself. The phrase, rooted in the Gospel of Jesus, is "the Signs of the Times".

It is a matter of simple historical knowledge that John XXIII encountered certain blocs of disagreement, amongst those hierarchically close to him, when he announced the idea of a Council. The disagreement gathered force as the preparatory work for the Council got under way. I am sure that the forces of opposition had their theological reasons and arguments, but in any institution the dividing line between, on the one hand, its historical theory and the sincerity of the guardians of that theory and, on the other, the desire to hold on to the *status quo* for its own sake and an anxiety about an unknown future, is very thin indeed. The Church as institution is no exception to this dilemma.

Thus an opposition to a new interpretation of the relationship between world and Church, as set out in the *Constitution on the Church in the Modern World*, was inevitable.[6] Of course, there must be a process of discernment, but one must not use either the need for discernment or the prolongation of its process as an escape route from bold and risk-filled commitments in the name of the Gospel, the glory of God and the world's betterment. From the believer's point of view, whether that belief belongs only to God or to God mediated through the Church, movements within the world or society tend to be perceived as essentially belonging to philosophy or some contemporary ideology and only accidentally to God. Such an attitude not only operates against the perpetual creative action of God, but prevents fruitful dialogue and serious conversation at the heart of the world. For example, the question of the laity and the development of ministry on new patterns should not be seen as "letting in" those who have been excluded from certain forms of Christian life, but rather a way chosen by the Church to struggle with the task of humanity's development, betterment and liberation. There is a sense, then, in which not only does the Church call to the world in the name of God but much more does the world call to the Church in the name of God. Whilst it may be true that a phrase like "the Signs of the Times" is a piece of ecclesiastical language arising from the Christian's contemporary perception of the world, and to be welcomed on that account, it should also be understood as flowing from a world which is announcing to the Church that certain inherited certitudes are collapsing or have collapsed. They are collapsing not because of some form of unruly ideology but because of changes in the self-awareness of humanity. This may be disturbing both to society and to the Church, but we ignore it at our peril and this could become the unwilling cause of violence. I repeat: of course there must be discernment, but I would want us to be clear that we are discerning the presence or absence of the will of God in such proclamations of a new self-awareness, and not simply examining the proclamations to see if they are in accord with our preconceived understanding of God and the Church. This is a real anxiety I have about the Church, the priesthood and the religious life today.

The expression "the Signs of the Times" should not be understood simply as "new insights"; it should not be debated solely at a high level of philosophical or theological critique; certainly, it should not be understood as a vast conversion in the hearts and souls of part of the human family. There has been a collapse of certain inherited certitudes, but the voice of God is in that collapse, some of the human family have not simply prayed, "Let thy people go . . . Set free thy people", but have said, "We are breaking our chains of inherited captivity." The name of God has been spoken, "I Am."

It is important for me to make something very clear: such an attitude of Christianity, be it encouraged or expressed amongst those who loosely adhere to Christian values or who are within the institutional Church in itself, is not a summons for Christians and/or the institutional Church to adopt a particular format of political, economic, social or cultural thought or philosophy. It is about taking seriously movements within society and being ready to discuss and implement inherited Christian values within the context and tendencies of such movements. But at the same time there is an obligation for the Christian community to make clear that certain political, economic, social and cultural views of life create an overall atmosphere within society which leads to an acceptance, however unconscious or implicit it may be, of selfishness in human existence, which only leads to a world of loveless competitiveness.

The junction of Inner City where I arrived some years ago I do not now perceive as a junction for a personal new world of apostolate or a new mode of priestly and religious life existence. I rather perceive it as a starting point, a source, a beginning for a major new apologetic for the Gospel of Jesus and Christianity. Social action groups, justice and peace groups, not to mention certain groups of religious and lay people committed to the task of human liberation, are not merely good things to have in the Church of our times, they are radically necessary for the development and progress of the Christian contemporary and future mission. They are the concrete response to "the Signs of the Times", and these "Signs of the Times" constitute a mediation of God. If this is accepted, not only will there be an authentic response of the Church to a contemporary mediation of God, but we shall also find a spiritual and theological revolution in the Christian community. This will take place, indeed has taken place, in many Christian groupings, because a distinctive and existential mode of Gospel rediscovery and conversion will come to influence Christian values and life-style. The basis of this conversion will be a quest for a union with God on a new understanding of the Golgotha God and a new assimilation of the hopefulness of the Risen Lord. Let us return, then, to John's "Signs of the Times", which, I suggest, offers a new basis for conversation with the world – a conversation leading to ultimate transforming action.

I need to quote two passages, the first from the document convoking the Council, *Humanae Salutis* (25 December 1961):

Indeed, we make ours the recommendation of Jesus that one should know how to distinguish the "signs of the times" [Matthew 16:4], and we seem to see now, in the midst of so much darkness, a few indications which augur well for the fate of the Church and of humanity.[7]

My second quotation, from the encyclical *Pacem in Terris*, is much longer and somewhat problematic.

The period through which we are living has three characteristics.

First, we can see that there has been a gradual improvement in the social and economic condition of the working class. They began by claiming their rights in this sphere; then they made progress politically and finally turned their attention to securing more of the benefits of civilisation. So that now, everywhere, working men are refusing to be treated as robots without reason and wills of their own to be used as tools by others. Instead they demand to be treated as human beings in every area of society – the economic and social area, in politics and in the world of learning and culture.

Secondly, the participation of women in public affairs is obvious to all. It is happening more quickly, perhaps, in countries with a Christian tradition, more slowly yet on a widespread scale elsewhere. Becoming ever more conscious of their dignity as human beings, women will not tolerate being treated as goods and chattels. Instead they demand to exercise the rights and duties belonging to a human being, both in home and in civic life.

Thirdly, we are witnessing an enormous transformation in the social and political set-up of human society. Peoples everywhere have either won their independence or are on the way to doing so. Soon there will no longer be any nations dominating others or being subject to others. For the men of all nations are now either citizens of an independent state or will soon become such; nor is any ethnic group prepared to submit to rule by foreigners. The age-old idea which led to some men being given second-class citizenship whilst others were allotted a privileged rank because of their economic or social status, their sex or their position in the state, are now outdated.[8]

Powerlessness in all the areas mentioned remains a living, not to say nightmare, experience. This means, in my own meditation, that the cry for liberation in such areas, and very specifically and scandalously at the base of our political, economic, social and cultural pyramids of power, continues to ring out. But worse than this, the opinion that the cry should not be heard claims not only a political, economic, social and cultural rationale, but in certain quarters even a theological one.

REDEFINING POWER

Our lives consist in part of a web of interlocking circles of relationships. At the outset of this meditation I spoke of my own decision to become a priest and a religious. Though radically concerned with my own personal relationship with God, I came strongly under the influence of a web of relationships; indeed, they were discerned as a concrete mediation of God in my life. My parents and the family circle, the circle of friends and influences upon my life choices, members of a wider parish reality – such relationship circles, and many others, were at the heart of the beginning my journey, and this influence remained and remains richly alive.

On that December night of my profession I may have entered what is abstractly called a religious congregation or, more popularly, a religious order, yet in the concrete I was invited into a very distinctive and unique circle of relationships. On the day I was ordained priest I was brought into another circle. As each new circle is drawn on the surface of my life, it seldom destroys the previous circles, but rather interlocks with them. Sometimes the new circles need to be subordinated as I attempt to live with circles of previous days, and also a circle which I believed to be important at a particular moment in life loses its importance, as I attempt to take seriously the demands and the experiences of new relationships.

For example, the circles of relationships which have emerged in my years in the Inner City have made me ask questions touching not only my personal life but my whole social life as well.

Our lives, woven together or brought into an interlocking experience of relationships, affect not only the mode by which I live out life, but also the principles by which and through which I live it out. At the present time there is my circle of friends in the Inner City of Liverpool, and there is the circle of the religious community to which I belong. They create my social life and, in doing so, create my personal philosophy and experience of life, not to mention the theological and gospel values, which are at its centre.

What happens in such a living process – indeed must happen – is that the circles of relationships in which I live imply a mutuality of influence amongst all who belong to them. All of us are involved in a process of power-sharing in relation to our destinies and, indeed, the destiny of the world around us.

We are, perhaps, somewhat afraid of this word "power" and I often feel in Christian circles that we attempt to disguise the idea. I think our fear is rooted in a historical confusion derived from the compromises we have all been part of when faced with the demands of the Gospel of Jesus. "Christianity's stance toward power in general," Jean Elshtain writes in her *Public Man, Private Woman*,

> affected profoundly its attitude on the questions of power in both its public and private aspects. Christianity at its inception ... challenged and questioned the power of force, command and rule and demanded that such power justify its legitimacy. Ultimate power, *potestas*, was reserved for God and that was a power none on earth could evoke save idolators. The singular voice of ultimate power was beyond the power of man to compel or to capture for himself. There was another sort of power – *potentia* – the latent power within each individual for action. That power was to be directed to God's glory and to the service of the faithful.[9]

I am not convinced by all of Elshtain's thesis, but I believe her distinction is valid enough. My conclusion is that *potestas* cannot be exercised separately from *potentia*.

I join or am drawn into a specific grouping of people – let us say, the Passionist Order to which I belong. The group possesses its own mode of theory, structure and institutional-isation. The "I" I am is developed to a point of maturity and is called to make its specific contribution. In other words, I exercise my talents and ability within the group. That is an exercise of power. But it is essentially based upon *potentia*. At the same time, I do exercise influence over others within the group and I organise my influence. I would think that is an example of *potestas*. If both aspects of my exercise of power are to be questioned or, indeed, understood, I must give some account of the sources I draw upon for this exercise of power, and if we look at the sum total of abilities – that is, *potentia* – of the group along with its actual influence over a larger world, the group itself must give some account for its exercise of power and the sources which it draws upon. What and whom does it choose, why and how does it choose, its sources for exercising power? We all attempt, no matter how minimally, to exercise power. It is part of our creative action in this world.

My loving someone, for example, is an act of power. I can love to dominate and I can love to find an ennoblement of myself. There will always be an element of self-interest. And, of course, there will be moments when I totally transcend such self-interest. "Between friends," Aquinas wrote, commenting upon Aristotle's *Ethics*,

> there is no need of justice properly so called. They share every-thing in common. A friend is another self (*alter ego*), and a man does not have justice towards himself. Let two men be together; justice is not enough, for something more is needed, namely friendship.[10]

But no matter how we define it, even in friendship we are still exercising power, and the crucial question will always remain:

What do I draw upon, what are my sources, for the exercise of power? Let me attempt to exemplify this from my recent experience in the Inner City.

"Community work", write the authors of *Faith in the City*,

> seeks to involve those concerned in purposeful action to change their situation, community work is *with* rather than *for* people. Its process involves local people being enabled to raise awareness of issues, ensuring that the objectives are defined by the participants in a situation, attempting to understand the forces at work, discerning what can and should be done and by whom, and supporting those who have become committed to these tasks.[11]

If, then, I enter a group, I exercise power within that group but the source of my power is to be sought in the fellow members of the group. We are involved in creating together a social entity, developing a *shared social power*. This leaves me, however, with a further question. Though obviously the social power is the sum total of the individual power resources of the members of the group, are we all drawing upon any other source?

For example, if our "purposeful action" is concerned with legal issues or educational opportunity or employment or police/community relationships or racism or health education or betterment of housing and the environment – to mention but a few issues at the heart of Innercityism – in order to change the situation, the need for sources of power likewise increases. The sources go beyond the commitment and enthusiasm of my friends, into the world of the political, the social, the economic and the cultural ideologies and institutions which create the society we live in. If such questions are not faced, then we may feel that our power arises from our personal and communal raising of consciousness and from our mutual encouragement of each other, but we shall, nevertheless, not be able to face the real problem of power over destiny. The institutional Church can write reports into the next century, but if there is no access to such sources of power, we are engaged in nothing more than a confraternity exercise. Access to such sources of power means a change in those who hold such power, and the institutional Church must say so, not only in words, but in action.

We speak a great deal about political, economic, social and ideological power. I have come to believe that in the Inner City there is only one real power – social power. It is social power which enables us all to create the more equal and just society in which we wish to live and develop. The political, economic and ideological spheres are the sources of that social power. If one has not got access to those sources, then one is without access to the creation of this new world.

To return to John XXIII, I believe that the "Signs of the Times" pointed to the access to new and different sources. I further believe that it is in such new sources that the mediation of God in our times is to be seen. In the Inner City, God speaks through the marginalised and powerless in the poor, women and our black brothers and sisters. What we need is not some middle-class philosophy of self-help – we've had enough of that – but credible access to sources of power. In the country and in the Church I find that this is reduced, at best, to some form of social action and, at worst, into a potential promise dependent upon the benevolence of the better-off. Self-help philosophies can encourage the abilities and the talents of those who exercise, and are encouraged to exercise, their projects of self-help, but these are ultimately destructive without access to realistic political, economic and cultural sources. To ignore this is to choose a path towards violence. I am suggesting that the "Signs of the Times" identified new sources for the Church to redefine its own power, they must lead to a radical change in the Church as well as in society. In other words, the poor, women and those who suffer the horror of racism possess a power which will redefine both the Church and the State. If the Church desires this, then the Church must confront the State both in the name of its own credibility and the liberation of the powerless. We must avoid the trap of vague self-help projects which fail actually to lead towards a transference or redefinition of power. This seems to me, to use a phrase once beloved of Catholic Action, the only way "to restore all things in

Christ". Such are the grounds for a truly liberating conversation leading to an ultimate liberating action.

MOVEMENTS AND SIGNS

When, on that December night, I was received into the Passionist community, I was born into an association of men and *in* the same association, a well-defined grouping of people not only possessing its own vision but also committed to a well-defined organisation. But I was part also of a larger phenomenon. My genealogy stretched back through the centuries into the earliest days of the Christian Church. At the outset this larger phenomenon would be better described as a "movement" than as an "association", for the religious life, in its origins, was not without a strong element of protest. Wishing to serve the Christian Church, it did not separate itself from that Church; but unhappy with the direction the institutional Church was taking it wished to bear witness to certain radical and fundamental values necessary to the integrity of the Gospel.

This twofold phenomenon of "movement" and "association" has repeated itself within the Christian Church throughout the centuries. There have been stormy and turbulent times and times of great tension, which we must expect and perhaps, in the name of vitality, pray for. "Be not afraid!" is wise and consoling counsel as it comes from the lips of Jesus. As a priest and religious I believe in that Church and, indeed, have deep love for it. I likewise remain committed to the religious life; but as new winds blow, new demands are made and new horizons emerge, anxiety and fear are bound to find their way into our spiritual agenda.

The tensions which emerge have deep roots in the very beginnings of Christianity. They can be and indeed have been, richly creative. As I meditate upon my own life and the life of the Church today, I find a tension between the fact of the Lord of history, the Risen Jesus, and the fact of this same Lord Jesus calling for water like a dying slave one Friday afternoon. There are not two Christs, but only one: there is not a man and a God, but a God who became man. If the Risen Jesus brings me hope, the Suffering Jesus plunges me into the flow of history. And if I believe that Jesus drew his power from the source of his Godhead, I know too that in those Galilean days he drew his power from the source of the world around him. As the Christian community attempts to understand and interpret Jesus in the midst of an evolving world, it cannot but expect tension.

Movements and associations both within the Church and the world I must look to, meditate upon, hold conversation about, in order that I may be led back daily to an ever-renewed understanding of and faith in both the Golgotha and the Risen Jesus.

There has always been a relationship between movements within the Church and movements within the world. To take an historical example: the life of Francis of Assisi, with his creation theology and commitment to poverty was not simply the product of his faith. There were movements within the world of his time calling for a Church that truly witnessed to poverty and would be an authentic reflection of the simplicity of the Gospel life. In our own time a Church self-consciously anxious about poverty and powerlessness has not come about simply because of an internal examination of conscience. There has been a cry from the world, and many within the world, without any faith in the Church, indeed without faith in God, have sacrificed their lives in solidarity with the poor. When such human beings, and the movements which flow from them and the associations which are shaped out of the movements, call for a witness from the Church, they often say: "Of course, we accept your belief in the Jesus who is God, we see that as essential to your teaching; but we also read of a Jesus dying in confrontation with the powers of this world in solidarity with the marginalised." When I hear such voices and perceive such movements, I know that I am being called to rethink my understanding of and faith in the Golgotha and the Risen Jesus, which must lead me to understand my whole life anew. I may be challenged to propose a radically new religious life and new expression of priestly life and ministry. I must not be afraid of such a challenge; indeed, it is a major aspect of keeping faith with Jesus. Indeed, it is keeping faith with God, because God works through humanity, and I have an obligation to create the context for his on-going creativity.

There is, however, the problem of the prejudice which can affect our discernment. In my years in the Inner City, I have been asked from time to time to speak on the question of racism at various gatherings, Christian and non-Christian. I must make it quite clear that I have not taken the invitation as one to articulate the voice of my black brothers and sisters; they are quite capable of that themselves. I have simply attempted to articulate the "white problem". Audiences all begin, for the most part, no matter how reluctantly, by admitting the presence of a problem among the white population. But it always fascinates me how, as the discussion progresses, the problem is shifted away from the whites on to the blacks. Having spoken about racism as the product of prejudice and power, one need not wait too long before someone says: "But, of course, they [the black people] have a problem too ..." Before one knows where one is the demand of the blacks is ignored, and he or she has become a problem. In other words, I find myself faced with a quick movement into qualifications. If, as I believe, there is a cry throughout the world for liberation from stigmatisation and alienation of our black brothers and sisters, the cry dies on the wind of white qualifications and self-justification.

No human movement for liberation is shining with purity and clarity, but before we begin our qualifications about the purity and the clarity, we should make sure we are hearing very clearly the fundamental cry for liberation and affirmation. This is crucial, and the same applies to more general areas covered by John's "Signs of the Times". There have, in recent times, been official Church documents affirming the struggle for liberation and the centrality of social, economic, political and cultural questions to the mission of the Church in its response to the contemporary world. In the world's movements for liberation there are of course, qualifications to be made, both social and theological, but can we not hear the message itself before we begin qualifying and parenthesising such move-

ments virtually out of existence? Otherwise we risk giving the
political, economic, social and cultural defenders of the *status
quo* a ready-made platform for the perpetuation of oppression.
If there is one thing uppermost in my mind in these days, it is
the vision of a Jesus who refused to wrap up his prophetic
message in a succession of parentheses. Indeed, it is this message of Jesus which, thank God, sustains a tension rich in
creative and redemptive potentiality.

CHAPTER NINE

Life's Tensions and Liberation

Have you ever considered the amount of waiting we do in life ? So often one waits for someone or something to arrive. It is not an idle hanging around, it is waiting with a purpose. And often, of course, one can wait in vain. The powerless of this world do so much waiting. As I have discovered in the Inner City they wait and "They" have decided, if only by implication, that wait they must. The Judaeo-Christian tradition cherishes the act of waiting. As I have already suggested, such a tradition is built upon a "not yet". "Christ has died, Christ is risen, Christ will come again". "We eat this bread and drink this cup until he comes again." "Come, Lord Jesus, come."

When I was a young religious I was introduced to four words: solitude, poverty, fasting and prayer. I should say I was *re*introduced to them, for they were words used regularly by many Christian writers as necessary for being a Christian. Now, whilst in no way rejecting the richness of those years of training, I have come to understand such words as connoting experiences or attitudes also necessary to achieve the fullness of being human. Unless I am able to possess time and space for an aloneness with myself I can never be myself. Privacy is not the same as solitude. I may need privacy to arrive at solitude, but they are not synonymous terms. There are millions cherishing their privacy, indeed, protecting their privacy and legislating for their privacy, but they have never known, perhaps will never know, solitude. For solitude is about the facing of myself and the discovery of myself. It is about me with me. And though it is about myself it is not about selfishness. Privacy can be about, more often is about, selfishness, but not solitude. Who am I? What am I? For what purpose am I? Why am I? These are the radical questions of solitude. In solitude the human being gathers himself or herself together, he or she re-collects the inmost being.

Solitude is about an inward journey. It is not an escape or a detachment from the world about me. But it is a finding of that world through my own aloneness. Though I look into the self I am, I know there is a summons to a greater world, and in myself I find at least whispers and rumours of that greater world. But if I do not know myself I shall never know the greater world. In this self, for the Christian or believer explicitly, and for so many others implicitly, God or a "beyondness", and the human spirit touch each other. Teresa of Avila spoke of the "inner castle"; John of the Cross spoke of a "house of rest in darkness and concealment"; Tauler knew it as "the ground of the spirit", and for Eckhart it was "the little castle". And there is a verbal articulation of it, there is an internal dialogue, for this is where the Christian steps over the threshold of prayer. Such are the fruits of solitude.

In solitude I face the nakedness of my own spirit. I will be forced, if I am honest, to strip away all my pretensions to arrive at my own allness and nothingness. If I truly struggle to understand myself, I will discover my dependency, contingency and frailty. In a word I am forced to acknowledge my ultimate poverty. It is a poverty which demands of me that I let myself go into the life of God, if I believe, and into the lives of the others of this world without whom I cannot fully be. Thus my poverty drives me out of myself to seek an enrichment in and with others. Paradoxically I must let go of my yearning for myself in order to possess myself. This living paradox defines my humanity and, in Christian terms, my relationship with God.

It is this paradox which also demands of me that I discipline my yearnings to seek their right and true orientation. I must starve myself of what is not radically necessary in order to find authentic nourishment of spirit. I must fast face to face with my own selfish hungering for a food which is no more than the "junk food" of the spirit. A physical fasting is the symbol of my commitment and intent. But at all times my internal dialogue must be dictated by a greater plan, as I seek to be part of and gathered into the mighty act and plan of creative love which, as a believer, I recognise as the loving action of God. Solitude enables the stripping away of the self in spiritual poverty to surrender to a larger life task, the discipline of the self to search for the true values which nourish the spirit, and the internal conversation, in which heart speaks to heart in anxious concern for the whole world, in which I become part of a sustaining and creative love.

This is not individualism, but rather authentic personalism. If, however, I turn solitude into privacy, self-encounter into self-preservation, discipline into a means for merely efficient living, and the appeal to be part of the greater world into selfish investment for personal success, I enter upon a path of dehumanisation, and I shall never achieve the transcendency which completes my true humanity. There is a particular danger today with a new enthronement of privacy. The urge to self-betterment, promulgated by a singular philosophy of our time, ends up not only in self-destruction but in the destruction of others. Far from being a liberating of the self the concept of privacy leads to self-imprisonment and ultimately to oppression of others.

Perhaps the current emphasis on privacy is encouraged in a world besieged by the fear of global death, consumerist pre-occupation, the technological invasion of the media and the obsession with information gathering. The old saying, in such a context, "You've got to keep yourself to yourself", may well be motivated by self-protection, but it is the ground plan for a philosophy of life, even a theology, in which doing is more important than being, having is more important than living, and the strong are enthroned over the weak. Failure or power-lessness in such a society is always the fault of the one who fails, and powerlessness is a self-created condition of the powerless. Even our sick and dying, in such a society, must be subordinated to balanced budgets.

The invitation of Jesus to his closest friends and collaborators, to come "away", to set themselves apart, was not an experience separable from the commitment to service. It was rather a moment to identify, perhaps strengthen, the roots of their commitment and to become fully conscious of the dangers involved in such a commitment. The mountain top experience was not an escape from the plain, but a preparation for the task of the plain. Certainly it was not about staking out a personal domain of privacy. Though there was a personal reflection upon and an articulation of that appeal to God, expressed as a prayer to the Father, "Thy kingdom come, thy will be done on earth, as it is in heaven", the God, Yahweh, could be understood only in terms of a mediation of God or Father in this world. The appeal, "Our Father", had to be renewed by the disciples in solitude, but the day would bring the sick, the broken, the powerless and the marginalised, and they had to understand that this caravan of human brokenness was their only reason for existence and the ultimate roots of their empowering. New inner dependencies must be revealed in the solitude of the "place set apart", which would lead them to a love for, and a solidarity with, the suffering of their world. If they must fast, then they must not fast like the pharisees. Their fasting must be a symbol of their sadness face to face with a broken world – broken because the God of loving equality, indeed the God of justice and universal concern, was absent from the politico-religious establishment of their times. Their solitude, their fasting, their poverty and their prayer must lead them to new sources of power: the power of the Father redefined in love and the power of the poor, of those who mourn, of the gentle, of the peacemakers and of those who thirst and hunger for justice. Were they willing to face up to persecution and abuse, even death, in the name of such a cause? This was not about a resignation to suffering or a consecration of those who suffer, but rather a commitment to giving them hope in relative and absolute liberation. He led the way eventually down that mountain of solitude to walk a path up another hill to die as a slave.

And in all he did and spoke of, in all that was implied in his invitation to come away, though he specifically called for faith in Yahweh, he touched the deepest and most inspiring yearnings of the human spirit. What he achieved in the "place apart" spiritually was implemented in the reaching for the masses, relative in his time yet still masses, in his life of preaching, existing with, and ultimately loving, those who surged around him. They became, though in a different sense from his Father, the source of his power. The thoughts of the mountain led to the action of the town. It was a cruel irony that the Temple police arrested him, on the night before he was tried and executed, in one of those places which were treasured for the opportunity it offered of solitude, the Garden of Gethsemane. There was no introspection in the life of Jesus; the solitude, with all it implied, was intrinsically connected with the field of preaching, protest, agitation and action. If the end came because of the ultimate challenge to the Temple power, and implicitly to the Roman coloniser, the seeds of the end were sown, indeed the causes of the ultimate actions were to be found, in the solitude of the mountain.

I am not suggesting that Jesus planned, reflected upon or gave depth of thought to an institutional confrontation at the end of his life. And, therefore, I am not suggesting that such a confrontation dominated his thought and conversation in the hours of solitude with his friends. But I do believe that he must have seen such confrontation as an inevitable consequence of his mission. Indeed, I would go so far as to suggest that his priority was with the marginalised and the alienated, and that to this extent he was ready to accept the inevitable – the inevitable being in the area of institutional confrontation. Thus he made his way amongst the people of his day, in such a way as to resolve the tension between that search into the depths of his soul, and the souls of his disciples and followers, and the demands of the larger world, by actions and words, born in the depths of his solitude, understanding of poverty, abnegation of the self and his prayer to the Father, conveying his understanding of the rule of his Father as a rule leading to the liberation of his contemporary brothers and sisters.

His friends and disciples seem to me to present him constantly with the tension between their own personal seeking of

God and the services of their contemporaries. They wanted *their* places in the kingdom; he had to rebuke them about their understanding of the relationship between master and servant; he had to make it clear that their lives were not to be seen within the religious power paradigms of their times, namely, that they were not there to be honoured in the market place; they must face the fact of having to give up all to follow him. The dilemma of how to look after oneself and at the same time reach out to others he ultimately summed up in the paradox of losing one's life to save it. In my own life, and in the place where I live as religious and priest, the Inner City, I find the resolution of the tension, the liberators, the harmonisation if you will in three realities of his life and activity. These are: his willingness to exist with and suffer with the broken and the powerless in a commitment to a better world, leavened by the values of the kingdom of his Father; his commitment to the purging of evil; and the very simplicity of his life in the meals he shared, which meant conversation, in the homes of friends and enemies alike.

Liberation is at the very root of the human quest. Indeed, it is at the root of my personhood, and my personhood is but the microcosm of humanity itself. But in attempting to realise liberation in life I must face the tension between seeking exclusively to making myself secure and seeking to go out of myself to others. There is an immanent impulse within myself simply to take care of me, and there is a transcendent impulse which seeks to care for what is beyond me. I am on a path of authentic liberation when I have organised, in reflection and action, the priorities of both those impulses. If, on the one hand, I neglect myself and those things which must feed my inner yearning in the name of going out to others, or on the other hand, refuse to reach beyond myself to others, but remain imprisoned in my own self-care, I shall never experience authentic liberation. These two impulses are, or should be, in a state of permanent interaction. In this interaction I develop, however, the "I am" which I am. And because I reflect, according to my human condition, the image of God, I am engaged in a godly pursuit.

In other words, our search for liberation is not, radically, a political, economic, social or cultural choice but rather a choosing of life itself. Though I live in and with time and space, I am forever struggling with time and space, struggling to control and even transcend, them. The ultimate oppression comes when the time and space of my life is snatched away from me and taken over or manipulated in such a way that all choice is subordinated to the will of others. In such a situation, the political, economic, social and cultural choices of others are imposed on me. I become imprisoned by the "They", so that I cannot be who and what I am. Here is the horror, nay blasphemy, of "Innercityism".

TO EXIST AND SUFFER WITH

Much has been written about the view and understanding of "the Coming of the Kingdom of the Father", as experienced by Jesus himself.

In terms of the practical conclusions which Christianity, in all its forms, has drawn from the life and action of Jesus, there often seems to me a careless attitude towards his actual act of existence and suffering with the world into which he was born and in which he lived out his life. It is not unconnected with something I have already referred to – namely, his Golgotha experience.

Whilst it is important for the Christian to live and preach the message of salvation rooted in the life and work of Jesus, it is equally important to understand or reflect upon his actual mode of saving humanity. In saying this I am not referring to the miracles worked, the devils cast out and the words preached, but rather his intent and commitment to existing and suffering with his contemporaries. The simple, though breathtaking statement, "The Word was made Flesh", did mean his being part of the world and the flesh in which he found himself. If eternal life was an important item, so too was temporal life; if immortality was a supreme subject for consideration, so too was this mortal existence – a mortal existence which too often for too many was a wasteland of the spirit.

Such a commitment to an existence and suffering with his

world was underpinned, so to speak, by a stark realism. It is absolutely true that the power and wonder of God's care is and will be with us, but we cannot run away from the reality of a world caught in the grip of suffering and selfishness. There must be optimism, but to use Newman's phrase, it must be a "sober optimism". To be sure, there is always hope – and that hope must leaven our every thought – but an authentic existence with this world must temper it. One may see this in the parable of the sower, quoted in all three synoptic Gospels (cf. Mark iv: 1–9; Matthew xiii: 1–9, Luke viii: 4–8). The seed of God's word falls on all kinds of soil. Such a diversity of rooting must not destroy our hope. But diversity of rooting there is.

> His doctrine of the inevitability of the Kingdom's coming is one that takes full cognisance of all the evidence that cries out that the Kingdom has not come, but still insists on the irreversibility of the providential working of God for salvation.[1]

Thus the act of existing with, and suffering with, in the life of Jesus was based upon a realistic perception of the world, which nevertheless has room for hopefulness. The point is we must see the hopefulness in the vision of Jesus, not as coming merely from God, but rather as coming from an equation of his understanding of the Father and the world in which he existed with his brothers and sisters in a shared suffering.

A "Signs of the Times" theology is the logical consequence of the mode of existence led by Jesus. This means that one not only searches for methods of appropriate apostolic action but also has to respond to a radical new understanding of a mode of existence. Thus it is not simply a matter of changing how we communicate the Gospel, we are involved in a challenge to the very basis of our mode of action. What the powerless demand is evidence of a realistic perception offering hopefulness. It will get this not merely from documentation, but from a sign that something is happening to the institutional Church which suggests solidarity with their helplessness and hopelessness. Indeed they must be able to identify a perception by the Church of the power of the powerless and the hope of the hopeless. They will see this when they observe the Church "exorcising" from the power structures of this world the evil which perverts them. The act of such "exorcism" is the second reality which constructs the bridge of transcendence to the life of the world to resolve the tension.

CHAPTER TEN

The Struggle with Evil

When I see the liberation of the powerless suggested by Christian writers as an example – amongst others – of the ethical application of Christian faith, I find it quite extraordinary. It is quite scandalous that such a term as "fundamental option for the poor" should be a theologically debated topic: in terms of the hopefulness of the Kingdom of God, there is no option of any kind, let alone a fundamental one. For the Christian faith there is simply no choice in the matter, a confrontation with evil and the identification and purging of it are at the heart of the human and Christian journey. But the purgation does not apply only to my own personal journey: it is an obligation to be honoured with regard to the ideologies and structures of this world and especially so, when such ideologies and structures oppress, alienate and stigmatise the powerless.

To be sure, on a personal level, we always live with a measure of self-seeking which is destructive. Thus our lives are, or should be, always caught in a process of purification. On a very simple and daily level I cannot find union with another, develop a personal friendship, unless I face the ever-present danger of self-seeking. And only too often, for all of us, there is the temptation to rationalise our selfishness. This is not to suggest that such an on-going purification process should become an obsession; and it is certainly not a programme for a pessimistic view of myself which ends up in a form of spiritual paralysis. But I suggest that it is precisely in the constant effort to reach out beyond myself to the other that I shall find grounds of my purgation. In other words, the denial of my own tendency to a form of self-protection, which can spiritually devour me, is to be found in my willingness to exist with, act with and, above all things, suffer with the other. The preposition is so important. That is to say, I can act *for* the other and yet easily preserve my own comfort. When I exist with, act with and suffer with the other I am drawn into the other's life agenda. Such a drawing in, when it is authentic, means a self-purgation which, whilst truly leading me to a personal self-understanding, stops short of unhealthy intro-spection. Rather, I come to grips with an evil which forever haunts me and sometimes possesses my life. To cast evil out of myself demands that I enter into a givenness to another. Thus there are not two separate processes, one which purges evil from myself and another which leads me to reaching for and loving another; there is rather one process which is the product of two distinct, though inseparable parts.

On a personal level, then, if the tension I have spoken about is to be resolved, there must be both the recognition of evil and the casting out of evil. I must struggle to exorcise from myself all that belongs to the reign of selfishness, and this can only be achieved by a givenness to the world which is around me. Such a taking hold of myself, in the face of my own self-seeking, in order to lose my life for the other, is the ground of my willingness to grapple with the forces of evil in history.

At the very heart of the mission of Jesus, without sin though we understand him to be, his own casting out of evil in his world, both in cosmic and personal terms, was his own total givenness. I can never forget the sense of silent awe which takes hold of a Christian congregation as it sings the words, "*Et homo factus est.*" Certainly the awe may be seen rooted in the sense of the mystery of God become man, but it is surely something much deeper than this, for the self-emptying of the Godhead made manifest in Jesus is a declaration of the very process I have referred to. God became man, existed with, acted with and suffered with his world, to underline, on the one hand, the spiritual emptiness if such a givenness is not at the heart of the building up of the kingdom and to exemplify, on the other, the wonder of a vision which has this givenness as its basic demand. Indeed, it is the root of all hopefulness. It is a statement which, in so many words, articulates the belief that "things can be better, that things can be different". In a despairing world this may appear totally unreal, but in a hopeful world it is the cry of authentic progress.

At this stage of my own priesthood and religious life I find the introspection of so many Church programmes wearisome. Of course, there are also wonderful examples of reaching out to that larger world, but I do wonder if we have lost some of the energy, not to say the excitement of, the "Signs of the Times" theology. Whenever the signs are somewhat ambiguous, do we retreat into a world of self-protection? I feel that this is where the trouble is. I have already mentioned this question of ambiguity and also the dangers of too many qualifications and parentheses. To struggle with the oppression of the poor, the powerlessness of the powerless and the marginalisation of the stigmatised, is to struggle with the forces of evil. To be sure, there will be times and events which cause ambiguities in such a struggle, but confronting such ambiguities may lead us on to a path not only towards the liberation of the oppressed, but towards a simplification of the very life of the Church itself. In other words, the Church's act of transcendence in existing with, acting with and suffering with the oppressed, is its moment of purification. This is to be found not only in its prayer, its penance, its pilgrimages, but in its identification with the prayer of the powerless, the suffering of the powerless and the journeying of the powerless towards a better life. One cannot leave the latters' demands of life to reports, sermons and specialised apostolates. The starving Ethiopian child brushing insects from her eyes may well call us to immediate acts of charity; she is also a sign of a divided world of affluence and deprivation. And that divide is a sign of the kingdom of Satan.

The movements of liberation amongst the powerless of our world, with all their ambiguities, signify an energy born of utter frustration to utter the name, "I am". They also offer the world, and especially the Christian world, not simply a new context for the formulation of a Christian social doctrine, but rather a bleak picture of the landscape of contemporary evil. Having received that picture, perhaps having had it thrust into our hands, we must hang it in the galleries of our speculative and pastoral theologies, gaze at it day by day, in order to deepen, motivate and determine our mode of existence with, action with and suffering with, the powerless in their struggle for liberation.

TRANSITION FROM EVIL TO LOVE

The junction of the Inner City, in my journey as priest and religious, has brought me a certain sense of bewilderment. The *word* bewilderment comes from the verb to bewilder, "to lose in pathless places". In using this term I do not speak of myself, but my sense of the "lostness in pathless places" experienced by those who are marginalised in our world. But I am bewildered, in a world with so many resources, by the phenomenon of their bewilderment. The Inner City population is that sector of society which is

> placed at a disadvantage by law, by social stigma, by discrimination or by the changing requirements of the labour market ... The Inner City is ... of far more than local interest. It is the bombardment chamber where the particles generated and accelerated by the cyclotron of a whole society are smashed into each other. It is a very good place to learn about the destructive forces inherent in ... society[1].

The problem here is that too many people view such a phenomenon as an inevitable consequence of the pursuit of the good of the majority. But much more dangerous is the rider to this argument: God is made to bless or, at least, approve of this situation in a superficially Christian context. Avoidable suffering is made to appear unavoidable.

For better or worse, we remain heirs of that period of history known as the "Enlightenment". Basically, its philosophies held that if we could realise a world in which the human subject would attain control over and harmony with the forces of nature, we would all arrive at "the best possible world". And further, insofar as a God was to be invoked as part of this human effort, then that human struggle was God's will. The outcome of such a philosophy of life left the struggle, and indeed the definition of the harmony to be achieved, in the hands of the political, social, economic and cultural so-called élite of our world. As far as Christians are concerned, however, in such a view God is manipulated. Whatever the evil, they will say, good will come. This means that the racism, economic poverty, social and political powerlessness which are suffered by the marginalised of our society are blasphemously carica- tured as the outcome of God's will. Avoidable evil is projected as unavoidable, that millions should be isolated and left deso- late the consequence of the pursuit of a better world.

The consequence of this unholy alliance between reason and God is that those who call for liberation are portrayed as disturbers of the peace, destroyers of the common good and irrational agitators with no object in view but the simple act of agitation. They are seen as opposed to a reasonable political, social, economic and cultural target for society and, when God is invoked in rather vague Christian terms, opponents also of the so-called Christians or godly values of society. To soften the hard face of a seductive rationalism, those who are willing, find themselves called to confront such problems in terms of charity, sometimes clothed in the doubtful garments of self- help philosophies and schemes. In such a programme social justice slips off the agenda altogether.

The ultimate outcome of such a social and political vision is the victimisation, not to say the criminalisation, of the power- less. At the root of this process those who are the sufferers and victims become the constant topic of an unhealthy form of conversation: they are "talked about". This unhealthy conver- sational content claims for itself reason and, if the occasion should arise, the sympathetic approbation of God. The fatal response of the Church, in such situations, would be to make Innercityism a specific apostolic or evangelical target and leave the proponents of such a philosophy without rebuke or chal- lenge. This would be a failure to respond to the inner demands of a "Signs of the Times" theology and to realise that the liberation of the powerless is also the liberation of us all.

I do not think many of us, in these days, consecrate suffering in the name of God, but I do think we are still a long way off applying our more enlightened approach to suffering in a social context. We may perhaps seek some kind of solidarity with the struggle against physical and mental disability, but not with the struggle against social suffering. Whatever the case, the value of the struggle is measured by the criterion of "who pays the bill". Even in the case of physical and mental disability, the frail of our world are subjected to economic criteria. The radical response to social suffering can be authentically expressed only in an act of solidarity with the loneliness and desolateness of those who are socially marginalised, stigmatised, alienated and discriminated against within our inherited paradigms of power.

Too often, in the Christian pilgrimage, the struggle with evil has been perceived and defined within the boundaries of personal failure, accountability, contrition and penance. One must not, of course, attempt to escape the essential personal nature of evil. Systems did not light the crematoria of Auschwitz – human wills and hands were needed. But the logic of those systems was so structured that the system justified, and indeed motivated, the human beings who perpetrated the crimes. In other words, though at the root of all human action one finds human beings, the energising force in creating a system is a philosophy and a mode of action. One may, indeed, go through a personal conversion of heart in life, but if the evil from which I am converted is rooted in a specific system or structure, the system and structure must also be dismantled. If we live in a system which agrees, at least implicitly, that, in order to prosper, certain levels of powerlessness are unavoidable, then I must struggle against the system itself. To reduce the whole problem to the conversion of individual human hearts results in a failure to resolve the tension between my own personal struggle for liberation and the demand upon me to join hands with the powerless in their struggle for liberation from social powerlessness. The struggle is against and concerns an evil which engulfs us all and is rooted in inherited ideologies and institutions which secure and perpetuate a system of social power with exclusive access to political, economic and cultural resources. I must seek union with God in a union with those who socially suffer; that act of union must purge me of my self-seeking and self-securing; and, at a much deeper level, their struggle for liberation must become a moment in God's grace which illuminates for me the choice of more profound human and Christian values. I must seek to "exist with, suffer with and act with" the oppressed in the cause of their liberation. In Gospel language I must make a transition from personal and social evil to personal and social love.

CHAPTER ELEVEN

The Silence of the Inner City

In the summer of 1981 the United Kingdom witnessed three Inner City areas explode in violence. The cities were London, Bristol and Liverpool. In media language the riots have gone down in history as Brixton, St Paul's and Toxteth. The stories have been well told and I have no intention of telling the stories again.

In June 1977, before the riots, the, then, Government had published a White Paper on the Inner City. It is worth quoting from.

> Many of the inner areas surrounding the centres of our cities suffer, in a marked way and to an unacceptable extent, from economic decline, physical decay and adverse social conditions. The Inner Area Studies of parts of Liverpool, Birmingham and Lambeth – major studies over four years – and the West Central Scotland Study in relation to Glasgow, have underlined the erosion of the inner area economy and the shortage of private investment which might assist the processes of regeneration. They have demonstrated the prevalence of poverty, poor environment and bad housing conditions, and they have analysed the response of the Government. They have also illustrated the differences which exist between the cities studied ...
>
> Inner Area problems are a feature of many of our older towns but they are at their most serious in the major cities. In smaller cities and older industrial areas there are substantial areas of decay, bad housing, poor employment and social problems. Deprivation exists too in some pre- and post-war council estates, sometimes on the edge of the big cities. There is undoubtedly a need to tackle the problems of urban deprivation wherever they occur. But there must be a particular emphasis on the inner areas of some big cities

because of the scale and intensity of their problem and the rapidity of run-down in population and employment.[1]

About six years before the White Paper was published the Passionist Inner City Mission was established in Liverpool. At that time one did feel there was a will and some measure of energy to at least face the problem. Indeed, the Inner City of Liverpool became almost a mecca for community work or community action or community development. In spite of my own interest and commitment, however, I do not believe I fully grasped the significance and the implications of community involvement. I believe this was due to deep theological and political misunderstanding, or simply ignorance.

During this meditation I have referred to the pyramids of power, but I have also qualified that statement, for, in the last analysis, I have come to believe that there is only one form of power – social power. "Power is the ability to pursue and attain goals through mastery of one's environment."[2] To achieve this power I enter into, or I am forced into, an interlocking web of relationships. Insofar as those webs of relationships can call upon economic, cultural and political resources, to that degree do the interlocking relationships possess and exercise power.

The fundamental problem of community power in the midst of Innercityism, is its lack of access to political, economic and cultural sources or resources. This is not to suggest that we can dispense with community action and community work, but it is to suggest that those of us who are so-called "professionals" must accept the fact that we cannot be partners to or with community action without simultaneously accepting and identifying the dimension of change which must take place in the sphere of the political, economic and cultural holders, not to say manipulators, of those resources. In other words, at the very heart of the exercise there is a demand for a radical transference of power. This is a radical problem, not only for the State, but it is also a radical problem of understanding and perception for the ministry of the Church.

But if the Church addresses this problem, then it must

necessarily find itself on a collision course with the State. This will be especially the case when it confronts certain forms of political philosophy propounded by governments committed to privatisation, individualism and competitiveness. And then the Church in such a situation will need to question its own nature and the reason for its partnership with the powerless of this world. It must make the radical choice between keeping its leafy suburbs in pastoral peace or entering into a revolutionary process with the powerless of Innercityism. It cannot have it both ways. If the latter course is chosen, this does not mean the abandonment of the former, but it does mean that the former must find its way to union with God in a new way. This must be the bottom line in all our missionary activity, spiritual revolution and reports. The Church, has moved not without purpose and commitment, into the Third World, but there is no radical solidarity with the powerless of the Third World without a radical solidarity, no matter what the ambiguities may be, with the powerless of the so-called First World.

Whatever else Liberation Theology did succeed in, it did succeed in making one point very clear: the progress and development of the values of God in society demand an openness to the voice of God, the mediatorship of God, in the suffering of the poor. The institutional Church must allow itself to be questioned by that suffering. Moreover, the phenomena of oppression do not simply call for a new permutation of the inherited modes by which the Church encounters oppression, rather the Church is asked to reflect upon its own self-understanding and attitude towards the social and political *status quo*.

There is a disturbing side to the ruling political ideology of the United Kingdom, namely, that politics are the exclusive prerogative of politicians, and that if those who have been historically perceived as outside the active political forum enter into the political argument, they are denying or disgracing their inheritance. In such an ideology, this is only the case, of course, when they disturb the *status quo* of that ideology. In such a paradigm of power an alliance between princes, paupers and prelates is categorically anathema. Thus a Church engaged in and committed to all kinds of palliatives to unemployment, schemes for self-help and even charitably funded projects for the weak and the frail, is an acceptable face of Christianity, but to question such schemes and projects and, more radically, the values which underpin them, is to trespass outright on already acquired territory.

Too often the Church has appeared historically to be the supporter, or at least seconder, of such an ideology. Thus its rejection of the *status quo* must lead it to a profound self-examination. It is not enough that it simply permutates its mode of activity; it must question the manner by which and in which it exists, suffers and acts with those sectors of society which are socially marginalised. Having agreed to be in a realistic world in a realistic way and having committed itself to the purging of social evil in solidarity with the powerless, the Church must reject a *status quo* which perpetuates the condition of the powerless and, at the same time, undertake a radical self-examination in the light of such a rejection. In fact, the scale of political, economic, social and cultural marginalisation in our contemporary world demands, or at least creates the context for, a new prophetic Christian life. Long ago Paul exhorted an early group of Christians: "Do not quench the spirit, do not despise prophesying, but test everything."[3] The final words of his exhortation are eminently important, but there is also a grave responsibility upon Christians to make sure they are vigilant in and to a world which calls for very definite prophetic words and actions.

Where I spoke earlier of exorcism, it was to emphasise the casting out of evil as a prophetic sign used by Jesus, as in his works of healing, to proclaim the presence of the Kingdom of his Father. I have applied this prophetic sign to the life of the Church within the sphere of social evil, and I suggest that this prophetic sign is required because of the scale of oppression involved.

It is often assumed that the problem can be dealt with by specific apostolates, but, despite many official documents, it still seems to remain on the periphery and to involve no large-scale change in the life of the Church as a whole. I believe that the Church could be revitalised by a response to the powerless of our society.

My priesthood, as distinct from my religious life, was a key junction in my journey, but like my religious life, the Inner City has made me see it anew. This new vision does not imply any diminution of either my respect for, or treasuring of, that priesthood; but above all things, I feel that the Inner City has posed profound questions to me about aspects of that priesthood. Those aspects are the ministry of the word and the ministry of the Eucharist. The Inner City has become for me a new mediation of God, that is, it is not something or somewhere to which I have come so to speak, but it is rather a place where I have seen God again. If I then ask questions about the Church and religious life in general, I ask such questions out of this personal encounter with God, which does not, however, belong to any extraordinary spiritual realm or involve any extraordinary graces or phenomena.

To define the nature of a quest for God is obviously not the same as defining or describing God, but the manner in which or by which one seeks God does contain hints, at least, of the kind of God one seeks. Again where or how one identifies the presence of God by no means defines or describes God, but it does give some idea about, in the first place, one's expectations about God and, secondly, offers to others an opinion about God. I do think that believers in God, Christian or otherwise, have given God a bad name or have increased the agnostic and atheistic population as much by the nature of their quest for God and by their identification of the areas in which they have claimed God to be at work, as by their actual theological definitions or descriptions of God.

Surely this is the key to understanding those ideas Jesus had about the Kingdom. To suggest that Jesus died because he was a good and kind man who condemned hypocrisy and self-righteousness is to trivialise his understanding and proclamation of the Kingdom; but to point to his attack upon the contemporary religious establishment of his day and its collaboration with a political colonising power, and to suggest that this attack finally came to a climax in his attack upon the Temple, is to get to the heart of the matter. In such an attack Jesus did not oppose ritual or indeed the priesthood but he did subordinate ritual and the Temple power to a vision of life alive with a sense of love and justice and a care, above all things and causes, for those who were broken and marginalised in the society of his time.

When, then, I propose the Inner City or Innercityism as the place for an encounter with God, I do so, not to consecrate suffering but to point out that God is there pleading to us to liberate the powerless from the oppression of our times.

I am not, however, suggesting that it is only in the phenomena of powerlessness that we must seek God and that the only apologetic which can make sense in the contemporary world is such an apologetic. At the same time, the question of powerlessness must not be treated simply as a "concern", however seriously considered, to be taken into account apologetically in our times.

It is not that the issue of Innercityism must be taken seriously both by a teaching Church, the theologian and the believing faithful; each of these aspects of the living Christian community can gain authentic credibility and be witness to a true contemporary understanding of God only when the phenomena of Innercityism are at the centre of the Christian agenda. I do not believe that I exaggerate in this regard and, I believe, my contention gains support in the following words of Pope John Paul II:

> Consequently, following the example of Pope Paul VI with his encyclical *Populorum Progressio*, I wish to *appeal* with simplicity and humility to *everyone*, to tell all men and women without exception. I wish to ask them to be convinced of the seriousness of the present moment and of each one's individual responsibility, and to implement – by the way they live as individuals and as families, by the use of their resources, by their civic activity, by contributing to economic and political decisions and by personal commitment to national and international undertakings – the *measures* inspired by solidarity and love of preference for the poor. This is what is demanded by the present moment and above all by the very dignity of the human person, the indestructible image of God and Creator, which is *identical* in each of us. [The italics belong to the text.][4]

Not many months after I came into the Inner City, a friend of mine received a letter from a mutual friend, one sentence of which read: "I think it is a great pity that Fr Austin has left aside the things of the priesthood to take up social matters." Ignoring for the moment the question of priesthood in itself, the general theological implications of the words are quite frightening. And since those days on more than one occasion I have been introduced, not in a derogatory manner, with such words as, "a priest or religious ... with other priests and religious ... involved in community development ... in social ... in political matters." And, I must add, as the years have passed by, such words as "radical", "left" and even, rather amusingly, "revolutionary" have been added.

One wonders about the perceptions of priesthood in this regard. Can there be a priesthood outside of the social and political arena, personally and/or institutionally understood? If there can be, what is it? Does it float about in some transcendent manner over the comings and goings, the sufferings and the agonies, of society? Does priesthood imply standing aside from the major political, social, economic and cultural problems of the day? If this be the case, then priesthood, not to mention religious life, is about a Gospel of spirits dispensed from both the implementation of, and the confrontation with, human freedom and oppression. When for many years I preached the Gospel of the Passion, with all the hard things involved in it in terms of the need for conversion of life, people used to say to me how wonderful and inspiring that sermon was. In recent days when I have preached exactly the same Gospel of the Passion, but illustrated it with the evil of our racism and our collaboration with unjust structures, people have told me I have no right to bring such matters into the pulpit. Mind you, there has not been the same reaction as long as one issued pastoral travelling permits to the Third World. Oddly enough, my first encounter, as a priest preaching, with a God mediated through social suffering and consequently questioning my understanding of the Gospel, took place when once preaching a mission in a certain parish in South London. I was given a long street to visit. The street was made up of old

Victorian houses. House after house had been let out, seemingly room by room, to families, most of them immigrants.
Families of five and six, and in many instances many more,
were living in the space of one room with shared toilets and
shared stoves on the landings. The one thought which struck
me was: if they come to the mission tonight what on earth, or
better, in God's name, do I say to them?

At that time I was also teaching philosophy to students for
the priesthood. The experience also made me ask myself what I
should be teaching them. Indeed, how could I communicate to
them the dehumanisation which I had witnessed? That experience hampered me for many years, raising questions about the
need, not simply to change the lot of the powerless in our
society, but to change the direction of priesthood and religious
life. But, even at another level, one knew that liberation in such
matters could not come about simply by working *for* such
sectors of a marginalised world, one had to work *with* them.
One had to work with them not only that they might experience, but in order that we might all redefine the meaning of an
authentic liberation, upon which the freedom of the Gospel
could be built. It is only when we have suffered that we can
with conviction describe the absence of suffering. One appre-
ciates more deeply the light of the sun, the freshness of the air
and the softness of the rain, when one has been locked away
from it all. For as long as imprisonment takes place socially, as
long as one is marginalised culturally, made helpless and hopeless economically and politically and even physically bruta-
lised, the victim is not unlike Primo Levi's fellow inmate at
Auschwitz, who inscribed on the bottom of his soup bowl:
"Ne pas chercher à comprendre" ("Seek not to understand.")

But when freedom dawns, then there is an understanding
which is profound indeed. When communicated to others it is
poetic indeed. As I have already said, the facing of the
problems of Innercityism is for the ultimate benefit of us all,
but to participate in such a benefit change also is demanded of
us.

CHAPTER TWELVE

Community, Innercityism and the Festive God

I read somewhere once: "Every morning I brush my teeth in a valley that is 35 million years old and think to myself: 'What am I in a rush for?'."

Even if my environment does not spark off in me a sense of environment millions of years old, I must say that in recent years I have come more and more to reflect upon the shortness of the time I occupy a place in this world. Juxtaposing my own lifespan beside the life of humanity, not to speak of the natural world, is a calming, perhaps humbling, operation. To be sure, it could also lead to escapism. It is crucial we all make our contribution; but our journey in this world is very brief. The heart of my life's task is to be located in my essential role of stewardship. The "I am" I am is daily called to reach for eternity and at the same time care for the time and space I use and occupy. Our obligation in life must be to hand on improved, if possible, the world we have been graciously given at our birth. The power I have been given over life, not to mention the opportunities I may have been given to exercise that power, is about one thing: have I honoured my obligations to posterity? Will an unknown future bless or curse my contribution? Will an unknown future be grateful for my journey? Whatever the technical definition may be of community, human community in all its manifestations is about my use of power, not only in terms of honouring a past and a present, but also planting a worthwhile harvest to be reaped by future generations. In a word, community is, by its very nature, orientated towards the future. Obsession with the past imprisons me in a sterile conservatism; obsession with the present easily locks me into a depressive radicalism. I feel I am freed from such obsessions only when I attempt to live with and act for a hopeful future. To achieve this, I believe, I am always called to save the "I am" from a depressive functionalisation. The "I am" I am must control whatever functionalism it is called upon to assume in life. Spiritual suicide rests in functionalism controlling and defining the "I am" I am.

When I now reflect upon my own priesthood two thoughts, are uppermost. The first is that I belong to an ancient historical heritage, a heritage which even pre-dates Christianity. For men and women have, century after century, searched for people and things to express what they believe to be radically sacred in human life. Their search has essentially never been simply about the person as individual, but about persons as members of the human community. My Christian priesthood cannot be understood unless it is set within community. This is not an organisational matter, it is above all things a philosophical and theological issue.

My second thought is that one major, if not the major, impact which my Inner City junction has had upon me, is the sense of the communal in a new understanding, perhaps redis-covery, of priesthood. This has come about, not so much out of theological analysis, though that has not been absent, but out of the radical struggle and cry for liberation, which emerges from the Inner City. In such a context, Inner City is not a concern, it is not "something" to which the Church goes in its ministry, rather it calls the Church to a self-reflection. To recall earlier words, "Church of God, what do you say of yourself?" comes from the lips of the powerless.

There is a problem deeply involved in the historical process of what we call the "vocation" to priesthood and religious life. To be sure, there has been, in recent times, rich theological reflection in the area of vocation. The Christian approach remains highly personalised, but my own mind has turned more and more in recent years to the demand upon me to give back, so to speak, my vocation as priest and religious to the people. This demand to give it back is not rooted in a matter of personal choice, but in my beginning to become conscious of the fact that, in doing so, I am only returning it to what or where, in part, it came from.

This is a profound theological concept. To be sure, I may speak of God addressing my own personal spirit, so that there is an aloneness of our relationship with God. But – and this has been a major theme of these pages – God's word to me is mediated. Vocation to the priesthood is not mediated simply through family, friends and other local people – it is much deeper than that. God spoke to me by calling me through the Christian community. Thus the exercise of priesthood cannot after that call, take place without my sensitivity towards and awareness of the Christian community. But since the Church is, in its sacramental nature and existence and action, the servant of the world (a point made clear in the *Lumen Gentium* of Vatican II), so there is a sense in which the whole human community, implicitly or explicitly, also summons me and possesses rights over me. And though I must exercise, when called upon to do so, inherited functions which belong to priesthood, there is a very deep sense in which the Christian community specifically, and the whole human community generally, determine my on-going action as a priest and as a religious. In a word, my vocation has its roots, and is intimately involved, in the people. This does not flow simply from what the priesthood or religious life is, it flows from what the Church itself is. If I do not grasp and so "exist and suffer and act with" the people there is a grave danger of a very dangerous process of professionalisation taking over.

Many contemporary reflections upon the inner City, both political and theological, present Inner City as something to be "worked at" or "singled out for concern" or made into "specialised projects". This is what I meant when I said to the Archbishop of Canterbury's Commission on Urban Priority Areas, "Don't ask what the Church can do for the Inner City; ask what the Inner City can do for the Church."[1] A "Sign of the Times" theology must lead, not only to a reflection upon "what the Church should do at and in a specifically critical junction of history", but to a reflection upon "what the

Church must be at and in a specifically critical junction of history". It is not a matter of a holding operation in an historical moment, but of a mode of existence and action in an, as yet, unexperienced future.

When I suggest that the Inner City demands a self-reflection within and by the Church, I do not do so because I believe the Church will, therefore, come to something new within itself. It is rather a question of reviewing what is there already in order both to exist and to act in a new mode. Thus if, returning to what has been a central theme, I take the "Signs of the Times" seriously, and if I see that the "Signs of the Times" are about what I have called liberation, especially in terms of our urban powerless, the movement for liberation is not, in the first instance, a demand for an additional apostolate, it is rather calling for a re-interpretation and a "new doing" of what is taken for granted. In my case, that means priesthood and religious life are re-interpreted and "done in a new way". Moreover, Innercityism is calling the Church to re-interpret itself and act in a new mode.

Let me risk a familiar quotation from Marx: "The philosophers have only interpreted the world in various ways; the point is to change it." As a Christian I look at the phenomenon of Innercityism and I interpret it as a radical rejection of the human person's God-given dignity. At this point I am "knowing" and "contemplating" a truth. As I grapple with the process to change that situation, I am doing more than simply entering upon an apostolate; the process in which I find myself involved must lead me to reflect upon the very grounds of my contemplative and active commitment. Thus the truth of human dignity is not only known it is also "done". Consequently, I follow the path of *praxis*, if I may use that word. Such a path is not about knowing a truth and then acting upon it or for it; it is rather a total approach in which truth is done. The doing enlightens the knowledge of the truth, and the knowledge of the truth is gathered up into a "doing". Furthermore, the entering upon the doing also questions, even modifies, my understanding and knowledge of the truth. It could be said that changing the world must change me; changing me implies reviewing my inherited theories to re-interpret them and, when necessary, modify or even change them completely.

The roots of Innercityism are not to be found locally, it is a world phenomenon, the phenomenon of the "contrast experience". It is the absurd terminus of contemporary progress. Plenty and starvation, liberty and oppression, affluence and deprivation, mobility and the ghetto, mansions and cardboard-box shelters – such are some of the pairs which create the absurd "contrast experience" in which we are called to live, made more obscene because of the very road of progress we claim to have walked. In other words, progress has thrown up a culture of élitism, such a culture is seen as the "best possible world" our gifted reason has come up with. As I have already said, avoidable suffering is made to appear unavoidable. In the United Kingdom, which boasts of its economic progress, millions are alienated from their own creativity, the sick and the frail of society are relegated to the nether regions of political priority and the young are offered spurious courses which may or may not lead anywhere. Of course, some may say this has always been the situation, but there is a difference today because of the progress we have made which could eliminate certain paradigms of powerlessness. The year 1760 – the somewhat arbitrary date assigned to the event somewhat hyperbolically described as "the Industrial Revolution" – marked a decisive turning point. For it was then that poverty was removed from nature and brought into the forefront of history. That had happened on occasion before, when the decline of feudalism "liberated" the poor and threw them upon the mercies, not of a free economy but of a freer one; or when the enclosure movement of the sixteenth century disrupted age-old conventions of land tenure and created new conditions and opportunities of life and work. On each of these occasions the new condition was soon assimilated into the old, made to seem eminently natural, yet another variation on the eternal phenomenon of the poor who are "always with you".[2]

I make this point to stress the fact that, though I speak out of what may well be considered the local situation, I am also speaking about the global. Though I cannot take on the whole world I can only take on my street, I cannot take on my street without also taking on the whole world. As I have always told community activists, and there is nothing very original in the advice: "You must act locally and think globally." For the Church there are not, fundamentally, inner cities or urban priority areas *and* a Third World. There is only one reality: avoidable social suffering rooted in social powerlessness because of an absence of political, economic and cultural resources. Putting it positively, one may say there is but one reality; the demand and action for liberation by the powerless. It is not only a demand for action into which the Church must enter, thus extending its ministry, it is, too, a matter of bringing us into a new understanding of the Church in our times. If the world at large has, so to speak, "done its truth" intellectually and technologically and ended up giving us a world divided, at all levels, into freedom and slavery, the Christian community, in communion with all men and women of goodwill, must "do its truth" over again. This is to create a counter-culture, namely, that of the Kingdom of God, to reject the world's conclusion by seeking to recreate the world again in the freedom of the sons and daughters of God. As in all its junctions, the Church can seek this in the life of Jesus.

The longer I live and minister in the Inner City, the more I wonder if there should be anybody "professionally" concerned with God. That is not the same as saying there should be no priests, ministers, religious and other commitments to the development of God's mediation in this world. But there should be a grave and profound anxiety about the dangers of a separateness, about a setting apart, so to speak, which gives the impression of them as holding a power, which is not identified with the radical power in the life of the people to whom they belong and of which they are born. In other words, living in and by the power of the Spirit of Jesus or the Gospel is not a pious statement: it is, in the first instant, a description of the total Christian community and, secondly, if I believe that the Spirit of God is alive in the whole world, it is a description of the very roots of being human. Though in the Christian community and in the world at large the priest, the religious or those who exercise specific ministries, may be called to exist and act in certain specific matters of concern, they must be perceived as being essentially part of that one power of the Spirit of God equally possessed by all.

I believe this has political, economic, social and cultural consequences. In other words I, as priest and religious, must be authentically part of the struggle for human liberation. I must not be perceived as a "professional" amongst other "professionals". This is not to suggest that I have no specific tasks, duties, responsibilities, expertise and talents, but they must all be gathered into a belongingness to the people and for the people and with the people. The powerless of Innercityism, I believe, are calling the Church to such a reflection. And I do not believe that any theology of the laity can ever fruitfully emerge in the Church without a distinctive recognition of the positive contribution the powerless of our world is making in this context.

When I arrived in the Inner City in the early days of the 1970s I came across for the first time concrete examples of community work, community action or, what some called rather weakly, community development. In fact before I arrived in Liverpool, I did a course in Community Development at London University. The Inner City of Liverpool was alive with community work. I remain indebted to that era and the friends I made; I came across dedication and commitment, not to mention love, in the lives of full-time and part-time community workers. For me it was an experience of the signs of the Kingdom of God at work in many lives not even knowledgeable about, never committed to, that Kingdom. Schemes were launched in abundance, and at the heart of it all so many local people were coming alive more and more to their own needs and demands. It was a wonderful era and much was achieved, but, all too often, the professional, bureaucratic and financial god forced the community workers into a role of mediatorship on behalf of the people. The result of this was that the energy of the people themselves, on whose behalf we were forced into the role of mediatorship, was never really released. The powerless of our Inner City were not given authentic power over their own destiny. Though consultation abounded, participation in ultimate decision making did not become a reality. I am not suggesting that nothing was achieved, but I am suggesting that our pyramidal world, when faced with the powerless remains content with mediators who will keep the base of the pyramid quiet and submissive. Real liberation comes when everyone *equally* begins to define the meaning of authentic human living. When the model of this kind of professional mediatorship is the major model for dealing with the powerless violence is inevitable.

At the heart of the life of Jesus, as at the heart of all Christologies, is his role as mediator, but we must remember that his mediatorship emerged from a very distinctive position of belongingness. The Church as Church maintains and continues that role of Jesus's mediatorship, but it is vitally important that the Church does not assimilate anything into itself or become itself sustained by the task of mediatorship confused by a professionalism rooted in a model of social position and status. In other words, all expressions of its mediatorship in this world must be perceived in the context of that belongingness to the people. Thus it is good for the Church to write reports, it is good for members of the Church to plead for the poor, it is good for the Church to be seen articulating the suffering of the powerless and the marginalised; at the same time, the powerless must perceive the Church in all its expressions as identified with their struggle and – which is much more important – must experience a Church which creates the context for the release of their own power and energy.

There is such a thing as the "power of the powerless". To achieve this I do not believe it is a question of creating "new and specialised ministries for Innercityism", it is a question of finding ways in which the voice of the voiceless and the power of the powerless are made truly part of the voice of the Church and society.

When cities burn and the sirens of police cars and ambulances scream through the night, silhouetted against the bursting flashes of petrol bombs, I believe the ultimate cause of the anger rests in a bewildered people's desire to utter the name of God: "I am who I am." Their infinite yearning has been buried beneath, and oppressed by, broken promises, racism and the stigmatisation of an institutional and ideological "they" pursuing their selfish ends. And though I cannot condone violence, I understand it.

For they already have suffered violence, the violence of political pretence. As far as the so-called First World is concerned this is the most corrupting phenomenon with which we have to live. For this reason, I believe that any formulation of a Liberation Theology in the Western democracies is doomed to failure, if that theology attempts to root itself in the models of the Third World.

Political pretence is rooted in a belief, on the one hand, that the powerless of this world have an authentic voice in the creation and direction of society and, on the other, in the marketed philosophical projection that the apex and the middle of the political pyramid take the voice of the powerless seriously. Such an opinion is more often than not underpinned or justified by a socially comparative analysis, which by-passes the corrupting influences at work.

Thus, such statements are made as: "If you were in such and such a country, you could not or would dare not organise picket lines or riots." This ultimately leads to the absurd situation of the powerless of this world being eternally grateful for being allowed to oppose a legitimate, though subtly oppressive, system. In such a system protest is criminalised by certain brands of political philosophy.

Whatever criticism one may offer of such documents as *Faith in the City*, however abstract one may consider certain articulated forms of Christian social reflection, they are nevertheless a first step out of an uneasy Christian professionalism. They prophetically embarrass hollow claims of compassion and cast doubt on doubtful definitions of justice. They offer a voice and a word in the voiceless desert of the powerless. A Christian community or the institutional Church, whichever description one wishes to use, carries heavy responsibilities with regard to language. For it knows

God's Word makes and heals, not some things, or some kinds of thing ("spiritual" things, for example), but all things. God's Word makes and heals the world. It therefore follows that all words, all areas of discourse and discovery, of debate and design, are matter for our ministry.

One of the most radical disadvantages suffered by the powerless and marginalised of our society is their ultimate exclusion from the *conversation* which creates society. The powerless are the object of language – they are constantly talked about. And they are talked about in such a manner as to criminalise them. I have always held to the axiom that one must listen very carefully in the midst of Innercityism. At the same time I have become somewhat weary – and this was an experience one went through at the time of the riots – with those who hold power arriving with one statement, "We have come to listen." The crucial question for the powerless is, "When are we to be honestly drawn into the conversation?" For in authentic conversation one has, at least, the starting post for true liberation. A conversation, which offers hope of fulfilment in action and, indeed, arises from action, tests the depths of our sincerity and commitment. In authentic conversation we are challenged at a very profound level about our language. We are forced to examine if we mean what we say and say what we mean. And, perhaps, as Wittgenstein put it in another context, one comes to realise "you cannot help those whose entire instinct is to live in the herd which has created this language as its own proper mode of expression".[3] The language I have in mind is that language which vilifies the powerless and the marginalised and makes them the cause of their own helplessness in society.

CHAPTER THIRTEEN

The Festive God

The society into which Jesus was born was dominated by God.
Indeed, when one considers that their society had been colonised by the Roman Empire, God was the root cause of not
only religious, but also political, economic, social and cultural
tensions. The occupying forces and administration of Rome
walked a permanent cultural tightrope. If we do not grasp this
we cannot understand the social confusion of the society in
which Jesus lived. Its pyramid of power was firmly crowned
by God as Lord and Master; the power of God or the rule of
God was understood as flowing right through the whole of the
pyramid. For Jesus, his understanding of what is called The
Kingdom of God was intertwined with the hopes and the
struggles of a people viewing all things political, economic,
social and cultural, as related to that rule of God. Because this
was a central or focal consideration for life, so – as with all
major questions in life – there were schools or groups committed to the quest for the way in which God's rule should be
interpreted. Against the backdrop of the relationship between
the empire and the occupied people, this question comes out as
Jesus experiences being a pawn in the trial before the Roman
administration in the person of Pilate. "You take him and
crucify him", Pilate suggests. "If you don't crucify him you are
no friend of Caesar", the mob threatens Pilate.

The life task of Jesus was, then, one of revealing and explain-
ing the meaning of God's rule, but he did not confine himself
simply to an interpretation of the word of God eternally
spoken; he preached the word of God as lived out within the
confines of a specific period of history. It had always been so
for Jesus' people. The word of God had always been inter-

preted, except for very brief periods, within a struggle for liberation.

About sixty to seventy years before Jesus was born, Pompey, a member of the first Roman Triumvirate – the other two members of which were Julius Caesar and Crassus – had been sent to rid the Mediterranean basin of pirates. This brought him into contact with Palestine at a time when there was a struggle about succession to the High Priesthood. Pompey got himself involved in this power struggle and the involvement was used as an excuse or a means for Rome to annex Palestine. As with all imperialistic ventures, the conquered had to face economic oppression. That is to say, the conquered were left not only with a taxation system designed to maintain their own homeland, they also had to pay their share in maintaining the empire. For the contemporaries of Jesus, that meant, in practical terms, two conflicting sources of tax demands: the Temple and the empire. Jesus talked, then, of a Kingdom, the Kingdom of God, when the land itself was torn apart by a political and cultural crisis about the very notion of the Kingdom of God.

It would be incorrect to suggest that the Gospel writers tell the story of the debate about the Kingdom: they are telling a story about Jesus and his claims and his resurrection. At the same time, there is a sense in which all the Gospels, in differing ways, are the record of that major debate: where and how is the Kingdom of God? It is a debate which winds its way through history. How does God rule? Indeed, even when a God is denied, the debate goes on. It goes on, because in the very search for dominant themes or values which govern and preserve people in peace or explain the very phenomenon of political, economic, social and cultural co-existence, there is a search for that which finally unifies in the midst of inherited diversity. And there is always the search for the values which must inform the unifying agency or ideology.

For Jesus in his time and place there was no doubt that the Kingdom, as well as the rulers of this world, and political, economic, social or cultural ideas or ideals, could ever be understood except in terms of God. The Kingdom of God had to be a *now*, whereas there is a tendency in our times, when considering the Gospel of Jesus and his understanding and proclamation of the Kingdom of God, to futurise it, in such a way, that we turn it into a "never-never-land", as something "over the rainbow". Because of this we attempt to preserve our understanding of the Kingdom of God from any contamination with the harsh political realities of the day. We seem to have fastened alarum bells on it which go off every time a political, economic, or social question is asked of it.

It is not without benefit to remind ourselves that the vision of Jesus implied conflict and confrontation. This conflict and confrontation were not simply with ideas and spiritual attitudes, but with institutions and fiercely-held ideologies. The puppet monarch of his day Jesus did not fear to call a "fox" and treat with contemptuous silence when called to account for his vision; but, more importantly, he had to battle his way through much more established factions. The Gospels explicitly mention some of them: there were the Sadducees, a Jerusalem-based party that drew its membership from the priestly aristocracy. It was a "realistic" faction, in that it adapted itself to the political and military occupying forces of Rome. It was extremely conservative and, as far as the Law, the first five books of the Bible, was concerned, there was to be no on-going interpretation. The power of the Temple and the priesthood was supreme in their eyes – not so much because they were sacred, but because they provided a religious, political and economical underpinning of the *status quo*.

The Pharisee party believed, on the contrary, that the Law could evolve in interpretation. At the same time, allegiance to and fulfilment of all its ritualistic detail were supreme in their eyes. It is wrong to see them simply as opponents of Jesus – indeed, there was probably much upon which Jesus and the Pharisee party agreed. The Pharisees had little time for the acceptance of or collaboration with foreign influence and they rejected the occupying power of Rome. Though revering the Temple, their power base was the local synagogue. Then there was the movement of the Essenes or what is often called the Qumran community. They were élitist, seeking fidelity to the Law in contemplative patience and monastic isolation. And, finally, there was the more active party, active in terms of military combat which have come down to us as the Zealots. They believed in violence and envisaged the restoration of the rule of God through violent means. How far they were an organised group in Jesus's day is hard to decide. They certainly came from his region, that is, Galilee in the north, and they certainly emerged as an organised movement after his time.

But having said all that, it is good for us to remember that, as in our own times, "most of the Jews of Jesus's time were the ordinary, uninfluential people who make up the life of any country in any period."[1] At the same time, like any country and any period of history, the groupings mentioned were the power brokers, the setters of trends and the sowers of the seeds of ideology. And because it was the country it was, with the inheritance it possessed, each group in Jesus's day struggled to find and articulate, indeed to boast that it owned, the meaning of the Kingdom of God. Jesus seems to have cut through them all, in one way or another, to take his vision of the Kingdom of God out on to the streets.

One day we are told, Jesus

> went out again to the shore of the lake; and all the people came to him, and he taught them. As he was walking on he saw Levi the son of Alphaeus sitting by the customs house, and he said to him, "Follow me." And he got up and followed him. When Jesus was at dinner in his house, a number of tax collectors and sinners were also sitting at the table with Jesus and his disciples; for there were many of them among his followers. When the scribes of the Pharisee party saw him eating with sinners and tax collectors, they said to his disciples, "Why does he eat with tax collectors and sinners?" When Jesus heard this he said to them, "It is not the healthy who need the doctor but the sick. I do not come to call the virtuous but sinners."[2]

I want to return to the implications of the Gospel words above. To do so, however, I need to reflect upon some other words from the Gospel writers, remembering and recording the words of Jesus. The story is Mark's account. They were on the way up to Jerusalem and they were apprehensive. Jesus tells them that he expects death. Two of the disciples had asked him to guarantee them places, "at your right hand and the other at your left", in glory. Jesus replies in words demanding suffering on their part. As for handing out seats at his right or left hand, he dismisses the question. We are then told about the indignation of the other disciples with the two who had attempted to get in first on the honours' list.

> So, Jesus called them to him and said to them, "You know that amongst the pagans their so-called rulers lord it over them, and their great men make their authority felt. This is not to happen among you. No; anyone who wants to become great among you must be your servant, and anyone who wants to be first among you must be slave to all. For the Son of Man himself did not come to be served but to serve, and to give his life as a ransom for many."[3]

The death of Jesus, which he had seen as inevitable in the light of the conflicts experienced, would be about his vision of the Kingdom. It is interesting that Mark links this to the question of service and the rewards asked for by two of the disciples.

Service or servanthood, even to the point of death, is reward in itself in Jesus's understanding of the Kingdom. In other words, servanthood is not a role to be encouraged in the ethic of the Kingdom, the reward of which will be "getting a place" in the Kingdom. If you really want the Kingdom then you redefine authority, face to face with the world's understanding of power, whether you like it or not. Reunderstanding power, perhaps understanding it for the first time and living accordingly, is what the Kingdom is. And one should stress the words, *what the Kingdom is*. I say this because there seems to be a tendency in us all to define and understand God, even to worship him, disassociated from the Kingdom. Thus you may say, "I will be humble and servant of all to please and honour God", but that is to miss the point. In being the servant, in redefining power, you take hold of the Kingdom. In such a model, power is redefined by struggling with the action of servanthood. In servanthood you realise the Kingdom and out of such a realisation you are able to modify and change all your inherited theories of power.

Matthew paints a picture of final judgement. The description of the event begins with the words, "When the Son of Man comes in his glory . . ." In other words, Jesus is being projected as judge. "Then the King will say to those on his right hand, 'Come, you whom my Father has blessed, take for your heritage the kingdom prepared for you since the foundation of the world.'" Then the King identifies himself with the hungry, thirsty, naked, sick, the stranger and prisoner. The virtuous are those who responded to these examples of profound human suffering and alienation and marginalisation. Therefore they can take hold of their heritage, the Kingdom prepared for them, because they have already taken hold of the Kingdom. Their reward is in their very response, because their response was already in taking hold of the Son of Man or the King in human suffering.

Whatever the specialised debate may be about the provenance of such images of the Kingdom, this much must be said: the vision of the Kingdom touches the deepest levels of what it is to be a truly "integral" human being. Because we have so often functionalised humanity, because we have taken it for granted that certain suffering, social and physical, is unavoidable, because we have made such values as competition and status into our gods and even God, it is not that we have lost God, we have lost humanity. But – and this would seem to me to be crucial – in Jesus's vision that is the very way one loses the Kingdom of God and, therefore, God. As the strangers at the Ascension event put it to the disciples, "Why do you men of Galilee look up to Heaven?"

The power élites of this world, for the most part, don't mind you day-dreaming, and they don't get too anxious about your visions. But if you start saying you are going to redefine the whole meaning of their power, and you seem to have some credibility and following amongst the oppressed and those seeking solidarity with the oppressed, then you are in trouble. That's when the crosses go up. One must think up some new rules for the game without taking away the ones that are there;

they'll at least come under consideration – and "the They" loves everyone to be happily involved – but under no circumstances attempt to change the rules that are there or do away with them and, most important of all, never attempt to change the game.

Deep down I have always believed, when reading the story of Jesus's Passion and the disciples' abandonment of him, that the problem was that they knew he was not innocent in the eyes of the Temple authority or the Roman administration. That is the reason, I would think, that Peter went through a night of mental hell in the courtyard in front of the fire, eventually to break down in tears as the cock crowed in another day. Jesus had challenged the whole system.

I have said that Jesus took the Kingdom onto the streets. Happily, at one point, Matthew talks about sending the servants "into the streets and lanes of the city" to gather guests for a banquet; Luke sends them, in his language, into the "highways and the hedges". The point about Jesus was the manner in which he took the message onto the streets and into homes. But if you decide to do this events are no longer under your control: the voice on the pavements decides for you what and where the Kingdom is and what it should be about. Theological textbooks may well describe and define the nature of the human being, but human beings decide and define for us, if we have the patience to listen, what the theological textbooks should be about.

There are too many "no-go areas" of human experience, and there are too many of us willing to be the mediators for the "no-go areas", but there are too few of us ready and willing to "exist with, suffer with and act with" such areas. Jesus, I believe, entered such areas by taking his vision and interpretation of the Kingdom onto the streets. In a dialogue and a dialectic with those on the streets he did not of course, hand over to them a definition of the Kingdom. At the same time, in their sufferings, in their sinfulness, in their expression of belief, in their struggles to be authentically human, in their quest for God and, above all in their questioning of him, he found ways and means and language to communicate his vision and interpretation of the Father. Dialogue and dialectic with them were not contrived teaching methodologies. Rather, out of the dialogue and the dialectic he drew his vision and interpretation. For this reason one experience seems to become vital in his ministry: the experience and action of the *meal*. This was the radical setting for his interpretation of the Kingdom of God: in the Resurrection, and its revelation in the conversation on the Emmaus road and the meal in the Emmaus house in particular, he was able to demonstrate how the Father finally affirmed his chosen life-style. "Why does he eat with tax collectors and sinners?" and "Look, a glutton and a drunkard, a friend of tax collectors and sinners", signify much more profound truths about Jesus than merely a reference to what his enemies believed were unfortunate social habits.

Nothing is more precious, and rightly so, to the Christian community than its Eucharistic theory and action. And in my own life journey I look back upon that junction, nearly forty years ago, when I was ordained a Catholic priest. But I believe it was, and is still perceived to be, too personal a gift; and, it was, and is still perceived to be, too wrapped up in social status, position and power. To make such a statement is not to denigrate, go back upon, still less deny, the personal obligations of priesthood; but it is to express, on the one hand, an anxiety about the subordination of the communal base of priesthood and, on the other, to remind myself that the Eucharist, in itself, is meant to be a living symbol of the Christian community's active givenness to the whole world.

It is a fact that the Eucharist remains in practice a "going to Mass" and priesthood consequently remains the means of that "going to Mass" becoming a practical reality. There is nothing fundamentally wrong in this, but I am not sure to what extent the Eucharistic meal is perceived in terms of the Christian community in action. And I am not sure if it is perceived sufficiently as life shared and broken together, even life poured out together, in a joyful giving to the life of the world. In short I am not convinced that we see it as a celebration of the Kingdom of God expressing a harmonisation of "the interplay between pairs of oppositions", as Amira Goehr once wrote in another, quite different, context, "dream and reality, sound and silence, happiness and sorrow, life and death", which were Jesus's Kingdom themes.

I do not wish to suggest that I do not appreciate the very sacredness of the Eucharistic meal, but it is good for us to reflect upon what a meal together should mean; the word "together" is the key word. All meals are ultimately about sharing together and there is no authentic sharing unless we can engage one another in conversation. The meals of Jesus, especially when one sees the guest lists, were more than mere nutritional events. They were gatherings. His last meal, held in the old part of the City of Jerusalem, when he offered a means to keep alive "his memory", was not unconnected with all the other meals of his life.

The meal in the Pharisee's house, the invitation to eat with Zacchaeus, the meals at Bethany, the banquet described in the parable of the Prodigal Son, the wedding feast, the extension of a guest list to fill up the empty places – all were parables of reality and so many moments for expressing his vision of the Kingdom.

> What Jesus's doctrine of meals symbolises, is first, that the age of lament for the absence of God has passed, for God has returned to his people in living experience making it a time of rejoicing, and, secondly, that the presence of the Holy One has reconciled his people by liberally, prodigally, bestowing his graceful forgiveness.[4]

The meals of Jesus became offensive to his contemporaries because he seems to have insisted upon the "presence of sinners and marginal, unpurified, people".[5] Who decided that they were sinners, marginal and unpurified? For this reason one can never overlook the extraordinary ordinariness of Jesus's meals. In the light of this, one can further understand – the liturgy of the word completed on the road – how revealing was the meal when they sat down together in the house at Emmaus, the day far spent, and he had accepted the invitation to stay the night. Rows, arguments, debates, brothel women stretched out at his

feet with oils to anoint the to-be-crucified king and even slates
removed to lower a sick man into his presence; what a glorious
and turbulent world it was, the day Jesus took the Kingdom
onto the streets! Dear God, it has the makings of a "looney
Left"! And, indeed, what a respectable and rational time it is
we live in.

It is all very well to say that we live in a different world, but
how boringly reasonable it has all become – a reasonable
Kingdom explained by respectable interpretations to make
present a reasonable and respectable God. Such a God speaks
his words in modulated tones by way of complex and diploma-
tic bureaucracies, the word so seldom breaks out in that exciting foolishness with which Jesus shocked, and even angered,
his contemporaries. When I examine my own life, it is not so
much my infidelity to the ideals of the Kingdom of Jesus that I
find disturbing, it is my imposition of mediocrity upon the
Kingdom. The movements of liberation articulated in the
"Signs of the Times" summon me out of that grip of mediocrity into a new venture, a venture that must be marked not by
experiment, but by a new era of pioneering. The table of Jesus
must be laid again, the meal prepared, invitations sent out and
priority given to the powerless, the alienated, the stigmatised
and the marginalised. Then there can be – and this is vital for
any memorable meal – real and all-embracing conversation
about a vision and plans for authentic liberation.

CHAPTER FOURTEEN

Conversation

We all carry a grave responsibility to protect and preserve what has been graciously given us in life by God. At the same time, however, one must be part of God's graciousness. I would think, in a sense, that is what is meant by those extraordinary words, "Be perfect as your heavenly Father is perfect". I have been graciously given God's Kingdom. My prayer, given by Jesus, "Our Father, … thy kingdom come …", leads me to a realisation, by way of the very address to God, "Our Father", that his graciousness to me is caught up in a process of ultimate and enriching sharing. In a word, it is not "my Father" and it is not "my Kingdom" that I address and seek. It is *ours*. In whatever way God is mediated to me, the mediation is essentially social in origin and social in purpose. The image of God which is each human being's radical possession, that image which we have referred to as the *"I Am" of God reflected in my own "I am"*, can never be true unless it is seen as belonging equally to my brothers and sisters in this world, my fellow human beings, and can never reach its ultimate fulfilment in one without at least their help and care.

Of its very essence, then, the Kingdom of God must be seen and understood in the light of the social. The paradox of this situation is, however, that I can hold on to the Kingdom of God only by letting it go. I can preserve it only by risking it; I can increase its value only by giving it away; I can develop it only by expending it. Obviously, as we have already seen, this dynamic of living brings its own peculiar tensions. This is what I meant when I spoke about the tensions which must emerge when we accept a theology built upon the "Signs of the Times", as outlined by John XXIII. The "Signs of the Times", in other words, tell me how to let go, where and when to risk, how to give away, how to expend, the Kingdom of God. This is so because the "Signs of the Times" are also mediations of God.

Thus tension between preserving the Kingdom of God and risking the Kingdom of God in the world is resolved in the very act of giving and risking. The Eucharist is the sign of this living paradox. Jesus is remembered, and the memory is richly preserved, in words which express the giving, breaking, sharing and pouring out of life.

It is not my intention to attempt to deal in any depth with a Eucharistic theology. But I do now wish to reflect, however briefly, upon the liturgy of the Eucharistic assembly, before returning to the phenomenon of avoidable social suffering and our solidarity with such suffering.

Servanthood and sharing life in the life of Jesus came alive, as it always does in all human living, in the experience of the meal. To be sure, eating and drinking became profound symbols when they were sacredly, and very symbolically, integrated into the *Memoria* Passionis. "For this is what I received from the Lord," Paul writes to his friends,

> and in turn passed on to you: that on the same night that he was betrayed, the Lord Jesus took some bread, and thanked God for it and broke it, and he said, "This is my body, which is for you; do this as a memorial of me." In the same way he took the cup after supper, and said, "This cup is the new covenant in my blood. Whenever you drink it, do this as a memorial of me."[1]

The sacredness of those words has been preserved throughout the centuries. But I often feel I have lived them, spoken them and acted them, in a vacuum. Whilst committed to their unique place in Christian belief, and wishing always to preserve their sacredness with reverence and respect, one cannot remove the words, so to speak, from their human setting. That human setting is the meal, and real meals are only truly alive when there is also conversation.

The liturgical answer to this reflection is the conversation that exists in the liturgy of the word. In other words, the liturgy of the word and the liturgy of the Sacrament constitute the Eucharistic gathering or assembly; but the "conversational" aspect is so caught up in a pattern of "speaking to", "addressing", that the whole sense of the shared word, namely, the conversational experience is lost.

In making such a statement I would not wish to give the impression that I do not perceive, still less disagree with, the reality of a teaching Church, but I do believe there to be a radical failure to bring alive a conversation, based upon God's word and the word of human experience in harmonious reciprocal service. There is a sense in which the word of God must be articulated by the word of God spoken in human words. And there is also a profound sense in which the word of God must deepen human experience, stretch it to its transcendent horizons, when it is expressed in human words.

I am not concerned in this meditation with organisational questions. I am reflecting upon the wonderful and inspiring fact that the word, and therefore words, are at the very heart of our liturgical existence and action. It is there in the setting of the meal. These days we are so intent upon making everyone feel they are part of the liturgical experience and the action and how right we are; but we must give as much attention to how we do that in the context of the word, as shared and experienced, as we do with the Sacrament and prayer. The greatest act of marginalisation *for us all*, in the first instance, but much more profoundly for those who search for liberation as seen in the "Signs of the Times", is the control and manipulation of the conversation which is both at the heart of, and indeed creative of, the world in which we find ourselves. The powerless, the marginalised and the stigmatised in our society are the victims of political, economic, social and cultural conversations conducted behind closed doors, whereas the very nature of the conversation of society should be, on the contrary, liberatingly equal for us all. All must be participators, and wealth, status or position must not allow some to participate more than others. I believe that a Church which sees that the vision which Jesus had (of a table-fellowship as well as the conversation that is intrinsically part of it) is an embodiment of the Kingdom of God, should be able to do two things: in the first place it should be able to see the unique importance of conversation in the process of liberation and, secondly, it should be able to see the sinfulness of so many of the structures in our society, political, social, economic and cultural, which continue to exclude the powerless from that conversation.

Jesus made it very clear that he had laid down his own life in total freedom. He had given himself up in the bursting forth of the Spirit on the Cross. The giving up of the Spirit was not surrender; it was an act of initiation. For the Kingdom must always be about the Spirit given up for the lives of others. At the same time, there was a sense in which a "They" had taken his life from him, because he had described, perhaps defined, the Kingdom of God in terms of the marginalised and the powerless of this world. They were, first and foremost, part of the meal and, therefore, part of the conversation. In this way he put himself in final and irrevocable confrontation with the powers of his time. His conversation had overflowed into the discussion with a court of inquiry, "first thing in the morning", made up of the "chief priests together with the elders and scribes, in short the whole Sanhedrin"; and, later in the day, they having "bound and taken him away and handed him over to Pilate", the discussion continued.[2]

Where does power over life rest? And where is God to be located in this definition of power? It was in discussion emerging from a vision which many others have had throughout history. This is not to detract from the historical uniqueness of Jesus, but I do suggest that the debate was about an apologetic ever ancient and ever new. And I suggest further that it is a vital one in these days, because we have gentrified Jesus and, *a fortiori*, God. It is vital because, unless we attempt to place this demand at the very centre of our understanding of the powerless, or Innercityism, we shall never live at ease with Jesus and his vision of God's Kingdom. The question is not about how leafy suburbs will help the Inner City, it is about all of us confronted with the wonder of what it is to be a human being and, if we wish to be counted amongst those "who have not seen but believe", what it is to be a son or daughter of God.

If we wish to keep faith with Jesus's vision, we face a profound revolution in our lives. And if politicians believe that they can hi-jack this vision of Jesus for their own self-serving philosophies and if we are ready to rescue the hostage Jesus from their grasp, we will have to pay the hardest ransom of all. That ransom is an identification with the struggle of the powerless of this world, to the point of being marginalised, alienated and stigmatised ourselves by the proponents of such philosophies. In other words, we must make the powerless the major part of our conversation, so major that they change us. In this way they become authentic expressions of the liberation expressed in the "Signs of the Times". It is our liberation as well.

Blondel wrote that:

> It is good to propose to man all the exigencies of life, all the hidden fullness of his works, to strengthen within him, along with the force to affirm and believe, the courage to act.[3]

Blondel's understanding of "action" is much deeper, indeed much more complicated, than simply as an activity in contradistinction to being and contemplation. Action for Blondel is more about the totality of living. In being a human being I am in action. My existence, my willing, my loving, my thinking – all that I am is *action*.

The first time I read Blondel's work, over thirty years ago, I struggled to understand it. A veil was lifted for me, I seemed to find myself looking beyond or behind the neatness of distinctions, the detail of definition and description, which are so crucial for Catholic theology, not to mention philosophy. There seemed to me to have been, in my own training, both a fear and a rejection of all that may appear to elude precise definitives, where the poetic would have found it hard to survive. To be and to do, to contemplate and to act – distinctions flowed out in an ever-flowing stream, cool and fresh and tidy. There is no harm in such a mode of thought and life, but the problem is that such neatness can, if not stop you, at least make you hesitate about involvement in the bluster and chaos of human life. Human life, not to mention what is sometimes called divine life, is simply not like that. The "I am" we all are is tempestuous, unpredictable and, above all things, alive in *action*. When the "I am" ceases to be such, it may not die but it will certainly stagnate and possibly waste away.

The problem was not so much a malfunctioning of the formation system, but in an understanding of the Christian community as over against, even separable from or outside of, the actual stirrings and yearnings of the human spirit in the world. One often hears it foolishly said of the saintly and the innocent, "they were too good to live in this world". But one wonders at times if the Church is too good and too neat and too ordered to make any sense in the rough-and-tumble of this, at times stupid, distressing, careless, and often wonderful world!

One may feel that Vatican II has radically changed all this. To be honest, it did have the insights to bring about change, but I am not all that certain how far we have faced up to them. There is still a great deal of nostalgia in the air and a perception of the institutional Church at all levels locked in the model of being a sign to and for itself.

I must enter a plea at this point lest I be misunderstood. I would certainly not wish to be seen as minimising the pursuit of theological and philosophical thought. Quite the contrary. And I would not want to be seen or perceived as careless with history and tradition; but I am concerned about the introspection that still exists, the inward turned attention that fails to pick up the sound of the world's voices as expressed in the "Signs of the Times".

There is much current anxiety about, and indeed an attempt to reform priestly formation. People are right to highlight the need to rethink the relationship between academic theology and pastoral experience. Should we, in fact, be now attempting to rethink the divide between professional full-timers and other part-timers in the field of ministry? All ministries, I believe, should be rooted in a unified formation experience. It is no longer a question of sending people to get experience from a particular area of life and concern. Rather, we must locate people in an experience and area of life and concern in order that the location, the experience, the life and concern may form them. Christian life is interchangeable with Christian ministry: there can be no Christian life which is not a Christian ministering life, just as there can be no Christian ministering life without Christian life. This is not to deny that there can be different Christian ministries, nor is it a rejection of the pursuit of philosophy and theology. But it is an attempt to suggest that all philosophy and theology must to some extent find its definition in the *action* of the Church caught up in the *action* of the world. I question the model of future priests sitting in a seminary or college being formed for ministry and groups of other people sitting in a house in the backstreets of a city also being formed for ministry. They should be formed together – or better still, they should join hands in their common quest.

I do not believe such a movement or development can take place immediately; I am simply suggesting that it should be given very serious consideration, not because of a desire for change in the face of the mounting crisis in society, but in order to find a deeper way for the Church to enter into the yearning of the human spirit in the world. I feel the oppressions of our times, the manipulation of God by so many, even the temptation of us to clothe Jesus's vision of the Kingdom in our secondhand garments of mediocrity, have cut adrift the human spirit from its true spiritual moorings. The way in which we structure the educational or formational system of any institution or society will determine the way in which that society will pursue its mission in life.

The institutional Church will not be able to achieve an authentic confrontation with the marginalisation, the alienation, the stigmatisation and the neglect of the powerless of this world, let alone their liberation, as long as it continues to send future priests "to get experience" of Innercityism. There is a whole programme of development and formation for total ministry which will need to be initiated in the very midst of Innercityism, with those who dwell and work within it.

I must be radically honest at this point about something which haunts me, even as I write. "Am I being caught in the syndrome of the grand plan?" I need to admit immediately that I am. I am so caught because I am attempting to meditate upon the contemporary reports which have come from the institutional Church related to the Inner City. There are, however, two aspects to the question. One concerns the institutional Church's concern about, and move towards, the Inner City phenomenon. This is what essentially concerns me. But the other vitally important aspect is concerned with the actual nature of the living Church in the Inner City, though these both obviously interact. Let me attempt to say how I would like to see the institutional Church express itself in the Inner City, extending my remarks in less detail to the Christian community as a whole. The basic assumption underlying what I suggest rests in a term I have used many times in this meditation, namely, conversation; and it rests, too, in theological terms, on the distinction between the liturgy of the word and the liturgy of the Sacrament.

The "Signs of the Times", in the way I have spoken about them in this meditation, remain no more than external topics unless they are drawn into living experiences and articulations of action and hope. They must become part of the human and Christian quest. Whilst such experiences and articulations can become vital in mass gatherings – it is worth recalling the marches and dreams of Martin Luther King – they can realistically start and lay foundations for life only in smaller gatherings. We are all well aware of smaller Christian gatherings, sometimes called base communities. Outside of the explicit Christian context, in the midst of Innercityism, there are many groups and gatherings of people attempting to change the situation and struggling for liberation. They have their own agenda. And, I believe without qualification, that agenda is profoundly evangelical, because it is fundamentally concerned with the betterment, even the revitalisation, of God's creation. It is truly about the Jesus vision of the Kingdom, no matter if not everyone involved sees it in those terms.

I dream of a Church structuring its whole life throughout

the week, based upon a conversation rooted in the word of God and in the human word, on the lines of such a small group model. How many groups there were would need to be does not worry me, but local people would be integrated in the development and organisation of such groups. This would constitute the fundamental action of the liturgy of the word. The struggle of liberation in all its forms would be at the heart of such a liturgy. This does not mean that fundamentals of Christian understanding of life are to be neglected. Just as the colour of the tree outside which I am looking at changes as the light of the day changes, so do I see the struggle for liberation as the light in which I perceive both the inheritance and the present life of the Church in my times. On Sunday the major expressions of those groups would be communicated to the whole gathering of the Christian community. From time to time ideas could be shared with the community, but the gathering on the Sunday would be centred upon prayer and the liturgy of the Sacrament. I believe the latter to be necessary because of our contemporary understanding of priesthood, but also because the larger gathering can create a deeper sense of solidarity. It seems important to me, however, that such a rootedness in the smaller group must not be perceived as "alternative". I feel it must rather be the ordinary organised expression of the Christian community.

The uniting of all men and women of good will in a common human quest, articulated by the word of God and the word of humanity in the "Signs of the Times", depends upon all kinds of expressions of the human spirit in all kinds of movements, but that unity in itself is critical at this moment. It is a matter of how they all explicitly demonstrate their commitment to a new understanding of power. Christian life and organisation must involve new ventures, both theological and structural. This should not be seen as a radical undermining of our historical inheritance, but one at a moment of crisis in history when simple permutations of past thought and structure cannot cope. I am suggesting a mode of "letting go" of a deceptive security. No matter what disagreement there may be, I believe we should, at least, be ready to hold conversation about the situation. I feel sometimes that we have all lost confidence in our potentiality for creativity. Jesus's vision has been taken away from the street corner, the conversation and the meal, and we have found our way into a sophisticated and self-preserving vision of the Kingdom which alienates the "little ones" of this world.

I wish to make it absolutely clear that I am being neither dismissive nor careless with "magisterium" in the Church, the pursuit of theology, the need for philosophy, the reality of priesthood and the vocation of ministry. I am conscious of tradition, history and our living Christian inheritance. Thus even in the loosely described, and certainly undefined, suggestions I have made with regard to formation and training, I would want to reject categorically any form of DIY theology and philosophy. Nothing I have suggested is particularly original.

> The problem is not one (basically) of understanding the distinction between priests and lay persons but of understanding the nature of ministry and its many different forms.[4]

Without, however, disagreeing with such a statement, I would want to go further: we must have a clear understanding that all reflection must be rooted also in the human quest and the faith quest of our times.

> Is vocation a controlled, personal *attraction*, verified by superiors and then consecrated, or is it not rather the recognition by the community and its head, of gifts which mark someone out for the receipt of a *mission* by [consecration] at the hands of the bishop? And is not that the case for bishops themselves?[5]

McBrien so quotes Congar.

Let me quote the inspiring words Congar wrote to the symposium at which Richard McBrien spoke and from which I have already quoted:

> You see then that my theology is occasionally related to events that come to me from without, yet derived from an awareness,

acquired very early, of what I want to do: to fashion an ecclesiology faithful to the tradition of the fathers, to the classical age of the Church's life. The work continued. Then came the war, which interrupted everything for me until I took it up again five years later. But even the war proved to be an opportunity because it brought everyone together. I had the experience of comrades. When I preached to them, they did not judge me as a preacher, but as a comrade, on my human qualities, if you will. I was truly one with them, and I continue to have a deep intimacy with those who remain. Many have now died. We were very close, deeply bonded. I had wonderful comrades! That experience showed me that modern unbelief was much more complex than we had thought.[6]

Here I take encouragement from, perhaps no more, than a hint. But if what I am saying here, as a very pedestrian voice, about my own development and reflection as a priest within Innercityism, whilst care for philosophical and theological analysis is crucial, it must be rooted in the joys and sorrows of an age. And further still it must be rooted in those joys and sorrows, which seem to question both our past, our present and our future, namely the joys and sorrows of the powerless. I believe the same reflection belongs to religious life.

It has been remarked, and with truth, that ideas seldom emerge from a committee. Committees, or any grouping for that matter, may well adopt and adapt ideas, reconcile and balance ideas, even qualify and develop ideas, in a common pursuit, but they do not create them. Ideas are the products of creative individual human beings. Furthermore, ideas are interlocked with the human quest and help or hinder the progress of the human quest. And all Christian ideas, no matter how founded in what we call a life of faith, hope and charity, are also part of the total human quest. As Christianity cannot isolate itself from the overall human quest of this world, so the ideas conceived and brought to birth within Christian circles cannot be isolated from the ideas which are part of, indeed create and enrich the human quest. This applies to religious orders as well, which must, I belive, transcend their corporate distinctiveness and give themselves to the human and faith quest in the contemporary world. Since nearly all religious

orders have been associated with some kind of poverty movement, I believe that it is precisely the issue of liberation,
expressed in the "Signs of the Times", which should be seen
and understood as God's mediating action and word in the
human and faith quest of our times. In a word, I do not belive
there can be any more vital programme today for religious life
as a whole, and for religious orders, than seeking to discover a
new vitality by responding to the cry of the powerless, the
marginalised, the stigmatised and the alienated.

Such factors as shortage of vocations, lack of personnel, aged
communities, communities with many weak and sick religious,
have stifled the creativity and depressed the hopefulness of
religious life. The way out of this is to be found, I believe, in a
greater concentration upon the meaning and place of religious
life in the midst of the human quest of the world, instead of an
introspective, though understandable anxiety, in itself within
individual religious orders about their own future. Not only
can this lead to a betrayal of the world, I believe it also leads to a
false interpretation of the founding ideas – we may call them
charisms – of the individuals who risked faith and life in
making the existence of religious orders possible. We are sorely
in need of a very different kind of conversation.

General councils of superiors, councils for major superiors,
general and provincial councils of individual religious orders
are not in need of new types of organisation and structures;
they are in need of a new philosophy and theology, based on
the discernment of the very *praxis* of liberation in the midst of
our present human quest.

Earlier in this meditation I spoke of our need to accept fully
the Golgotha God. That is, we must accept the possibility of
the death of certain structures and tendencies. Certain groupings may have to come to an end when they no longer respond
to present crises, but I cannot accept that the capacity to usher
in a creative new era is dead. Rather do we need to accept
certain aspects of death for the sake of resurrection.

One of our chief difficulties seems to reside in our understanding of the "laity", which should be seen as our common
grounding. We are all the people of the world and of God.

When we choose a certain path such as a priestly vocation, we choose and pursue it with and through the commonality and communality of our humanity and faith. In saying this I am not offering a new theology of the laity, but simply suggesting that different choices must be honoured both in their inner meaning and in the light of an historical inheritance. But choices should not lead to a separation from the common human and Christian struggle. The historical spectrum which stretches from Anthony in the desert to a contemporary man or woman of faith founding a group in our broken urban world is rich in meaning – the religious life journey has been complex and varied – but, as with every traveller, new turnings need to be taken along the road. There will be new junctions. And, indeed, there will be need to seek direction, in which present advice can be as rich as the past. So the question of the laity's relationship to both religious life (and radically we should remember that it is historically a lay movement) and the ordained ministry must not be viewed from the angle of the religious life or ordained ministry facing crisis. It should also be viewed from a change in what the laity is and wishes to be and how and what its historical place has been. In becoming a priest and a religious I must not leave the commonality of the lay experience. My relationship with that experience may well be different and may call for certain fundamental decisions in relation to it, but how and where and what the laity is must be a positive and changing factor upon my life. In a word, like everyone else, I am still essentially part of the human and faith quest.

I suggest that by over-sacralising situations one de-sacralises them. Such a process takes place when social élitism is made an élitism within the Kingdom of God. Religious life did not begin to collapse historically, especially towards the end of the fourteenth century, primarily because of a lack of commitment to the Gospel; it collapsed because the respect it demanded on sacred or religious grounds was really a demand for respect rooted in social position, status and power. Thus many saw religious life at that period, based as it was upon social power and position, as a mockery of the sacred. Honouring a holy person became confused with honouring a well-heeled individual or individuals who lived in relative comfort.

The religious and, of course, the priests I know and with many of whom I can claim friendship, are good, sincere, self-sacrificial and committed Christians. I am not talking about individuals however, but institutions. I am asking for a reunderstanding of religious life in the light of the human and faith quest. In such an undertaking, the experience of what we call the laity must be the basis on which we move forward and, in particular, the laity of the Church and the people of the world plunged into powerlessness and marginalisation.

Whilst understanding and accepting the technical nature, theologically, of the term "the laity", I believe we need to emancipate ourselves from a certain arrogant view of it. All those people on the station platform, so many years ago – were they or was that "the laity"? Is Tommy in the prison with nowhere to go "the laity"? In the MIND home where I live, are the residents "the laity"? Is Jimmy, next door but one to me, after twenty-five years nursing his wife, with next to no nursing facilities, "the laity"? What about Jenny whom I buried in the anonymity of Springfield Crematorium, Jenny who baked scones for me on Sunday, Jenny lost in the files of a mental institute for years, is she "the laity"? Is my friend Paul, driven out of a pub with the word "nigger', "the laity"? Or, on more prosaic grounds, what about Jack, going out at eight o'clock in the morning, pretending he has a job, is he "the laity"? Bill and Joan waiting up for their eldest daughter to come home at two in the morning, conscious she is on drugs, is she and are they "the laity"?

I am not dismissing inherited traditional and theological distinctions, but I do feel we need a much greater awareness of the common and communal nature of our struggle to develop Jesus's vision of the Kingdom. And we should be careful we do not allow technical – though very valid – distinctions to lock us into a particular type of mind-set. We must be careful of this for a very fundamental reason: we risk cutting ourselves and the Church off from, as Pope John put it, "the primordial inheritance of all mankind".

Let me offer an analogy. In the world in which I live today, and very especially in my immediate world of Innercityism, I am more and more conscious of the patterns of specialisation, which I must either attempt to understand, submissively accept or agree to live with in a state of ignorance. I respect such specialisations and accept the fact that they are inevitable in a very complex world. But such specialisations can so easily build their own self-serving kingdoms and acquire in varying ways their own defence mechanisms. They can also arrive at a point where they tolerate no questions about their right to exist, the paths they pursue and the aims they achieve. Lay people lose confidence in their own reflections upon and judgements about life, a mode of dogmatic control takes over. Ordinary human minds are silently and subtly colonised, and our political, economic, social and cultural institutions can become the prey of such specialisations. Thus an openness to truth gives way to self-protective ideologies. To be sure, such has always been the case, but in a world claiming ever-evolving progress and power over its own destiny, the matter becomes more and more critical.

There is always a danger of humanity falling into the "technological grip" of specialisation to such an extent that any statement or reflection not fed by the ideas and unaware of the mechanisms of specialisation succumbs to an uncritical timidity or is peremptorily dismissed or even simply silenced.

I would think that the "Community Movement or Community Action or Community politics" emerged, at least in part, from this consciousness of specialisation. In the last analysis, however, they have lacked access to the sources of power because in our urban world the sources of power are located in specialisation. All specialisation must be the servant of humankind, and it is problematic to be a servant. And all specialisations must strive for intellectual honesty and openness to the voice of the world. Indeed, specialisation cannot achieve real servanthood unless the voice of the world is brought into an on-going conversation. To achieve this it must not seek some hidden secret, create some great mystique that will strike ordinary human beings with paralysing awe. Specialisation must be inspired, to adopt terminology usually applied to religious contexts, both by a pastoral concern and a missionary zeal. Its sense of servanthood will go a long way to harmonise the concern and the zeal; it will also keep it conscious of its own utter dependency upon human striving, attuned to its obligations of accountability and force it to combine great fortitude with authentic humility, confronted with the world through which it makes its journey. Specialisation must seek at all times to emancipate itself from a crippling pride and see its task as intimately interwoven with the human search for emancipation from real – however anonymous and polite – power blocks. The world of technology, the world of education, the world of politics and the world of social analysis and concern exist and act only because of *the world*. The "cognitive interests", to use Habermas's phrase[7], of specialisation must be submitted to the "backstreet interests" of the daily human quest. This is, I find, the most painful lesson to be learnt in the midst of Innercityism.

"Laity" thus becomes for me a transitional term. That is to say, it is a term which, gently though firmly, takes me by the hand, across the Kedron brook of human experience, and says to me, "Behold, the man!". I would not now want its technical theological significance to get in the way of my meditation.

Priesthood and religious life seem to me these days to be so often locked in certain paradigms of power that they lose contact with the turbulent world of Jesus's Kingdom. It was Rahner who once made the remark,

> In today's world, poverty and humility should be a thorn in the side of secular society and the Church, a dangerous recollection of Jesus and a threat to the *status quo* of Church institutions.

This has been a personal meditation and, therefore, I must ask, "Am I that?" I really think we should stop asking questions about the laity and start asking serious questions about priesthood and religious life. And if this theologically argued-about laity feel for a moment that they're off the hook, I would ask them about their and my broken, stigmatised, marginalised and powerless brothers and sisters. If we really want a new and different Church why not create a context in which the inheritors of Jesus's street corner, meal and conversation Kingdom are able to deliver it up to us? "It's not easy", we all say. Of course, it's not easy, but we need to make a start. So many of us say we need this kind of new beginning. I ask myself, "Do we want it?" If we don't want it, we really should stop talking about it and we really should stop writing reports about it. We must stop helping them, and create a context for them to help us. This calls into question all our colleges and seminaries of education, our novitiates and our "radical" pastoral and missionary endeavours. Mediatorship and professionalism in Christian terms will need to go to the wall.

This is not a question about restoring married men to the priesthood, recruiting more permanent deacons, ordaining women and training lay people in the science and art of catechetics. It is certainly not about giving lay people jobs in educational, pastoral and financial posts of responsibility. To be frank, we should be able to do a lot of that without a great deal of thought, revised theology or administrative re-organisation. It's primarily about the problem of sinfulness in our world and the emancipation of human beings from the grip of technical Christianity and technical society. It's about being revolutionised by Pope John's "Signs of the Times". Deeper still, it's about Jesus's vision of the Kingdom. The problem – indeed the threat – of Jesus, both for the Temple and the Roman Empire, was that he simply didn't want their jobs, he had other ideas altogether. Risen from the dead, he broke bread with a couple of friends and called others to the seashore to have breakfast. Great days! But we've done nothing else but look back self-consciously at his foolish vision ever since. We've accommodated tyrants, compromised ourselves with dehumanising values, said the right thing in the wrong place, the wrong thing in the right place and sung in wonderful and inspiring chorus, "*Et Homo factus*, etc". We are all human, of course. But that's the point, so was he: we've had Councils to prove it. And, thank God, we've had so many wonderful prophets and servants – they've kissed the sores of the slaves, bandaged the wounds of the broken, housed the homeless, visited the sick, clothed the naked, welcomed the stranger and – we must never forget it – pointed to breathtaking horizons of unity, truth, goodness, beauty, justice and liberty. The problem has been, far too often, that those who have been loved, healed and liberated, have not been invited back to tell their tale and show us the path of love, healing and liberty. They have been beckoning signs for our "action" to them, but they have not been liberating signs of our "action" with them for the development of the Kingdom. It's the acceptable time for poverty and humility. There's a critical century ahead.

I've had a wonderful life, which began in a special way on that junction platform amidst the stationmaster's wallflowers. I have been privileged to teach students philosophy and attempt to offer them inspiration for a future. I have talked with group after group of laymen and women about the Church's apostolate. There were wonderful days, and long nights, with young Christian students and young Christian workers. I have talked about Christ at Hyde Park Corner, Nottingham City Square, Derby Town Centre, Coventry Precinct, the Liverpool Pier Head and the Town Moor at Newcastle. There have been missions and retreats to the laity, religious and priests throughout the country. I have lectured on the hope of a new ministering Church, summer after summer, in the United States. I have attempted to play my part at general chapters of my own order. In the midst of it all so many friendships have been made and maintained. And, eventually, I came home to Liverpool, not many miles away from that junction platform. I came home, not alone, but with a Passionist community and life began again. So many new friendships began to develop. In the Inner City and the prison, God mediated all anew and offered me a "New Clock of Influence", at times frightening, but always joyful. I found myself having to face up to a different Golgotha and Risen God. That is all I have attempted to share with you. One very small witness in a great witnessing world.

CHAPTER FIFTEEN

An Ecumenism Beyond Ecumenism

I find God mediated to me now in the struggle of the poor, my black brothers and sisters, and women in society (though the latter topic has not been an explicit part of my meditation) for liberation into the fullness of their human existence by way of a fullness of participation. It is by this road that Innercityism has led me deeper into an understanding of God. The reality of the power of participation, without qualifications, in the liberation of humanity, is the final affirmation of both human beingness and the very being of God. And it is in the understanding of this affirmation that we shall find the energy to drive out of our world the dangerous idolatry to be found in certain forms of so-called enterprise philosophies which dehumanise us and dedivinise God.

And though I know only too well that the quest for the historical Jesus is an historical, biblical, philosophical and theological minefield, Innercityism has forced me to ask about the human context of the tears, joys and suffering of Jesus, because I have seen, and sometimes been part of, the tears, joys and sufferings of Inner City existence. Though accepting and believing in the reality of a redemptive Passion of Jesus with vast historical consequences, I would suggest that Golgotha was also a consequence of political, economic, social and cultural forces of oppression at a moment of high imperialism and colonialism. Golgotha was a radical question mark about the nature and exercise of power. It could have been located on any acre of waste ground in our Inner Cities. The Inner City thus becomes not only a solidarity meeting point with the powerless of the world, it is also a solidarity point with the vision, and the opposition to the vision, of Jesus. The Inner City offers a logic of experience with which all institutions, including the Church, must come to grips if the very wonder of being human is to be universally honoured and affirmed. Above all things, all talking about the Inner City must give way to a conversing with.

I am disturbed that all our reflecting upon a future of Christian ministry, not to say life, has never called on the experience of the many local people involved in the struggle to make the Inner City a better place. I have so often witnessed the fatigue, the near despair, indeed "the dark night of sense and spirit", which they have experienced. And yet they have still found resources of the spirit to point to, or call for, awareness of moments of resurrection. In the midst of a professional analysis they have offered a unique daily lived synthesis with which an Inner City population exists and, therefore, defines its existence. For me, personally, witnessing such lives has resulted in my being a "born again Christian". It has been so because I have heard at least whispers or rumours of, "*Et Homo factus est . . . Et Verbum factum est.*" At such moments a terrible and tremendous silence takes over my soul and I glimpse, no matter how briefly, the God who said, "I am Who am". I touch the garments of a healing love and understanding pushing through the crowded and mob-like customs and preoccupations of an institutional Christianity. I am reminded of the black woman pastor who said to me as we prepared to face another session one Saturday evening concerned with racism and the Inner City, "Austin, I get so tired of having to prove to other human beings that we also are human beings." At that moment the slave ships pulled out again from the dockside of Liverpool and the sun set, and simultaneously rose, over the River Mersey, and all our stocks and shares, balances of payments, privatisations, enterprise cultures and, indeed, Church enterprises, were dust in my mouth, as I searched for a word of encouragement. At such a moment the "Signs of the Times" imperiously demand a response. Will those people minister to us or do I simply minister to them?

The nature of our response will, quite simply, determine the future of institutional Christianity, for we are talking about the real thing. We are talking about human existence. We are talking about the living. The past offers us many things, the dead still speak, words never die, they keep on being articulated; but they must be articulated in the context of new demands. I believe the institutional Church too often lives with the dead, it too often attempts to dress up the skeletons of history in modern garb. Thus it can happen that the clearest expression of the very spirit of the risen and living Jesus, its song of hope, is drowned by the rattling of dry bones.

I will conclude with a haunting Indian prayer.

When I am dead
Cry for me a little
Think of me sometimes
But not too much.
Think of me now and again
As I was in life
At some moments it's pleasant to recall
But not for long.
Leave me in peace
And I shall leave you in peace
And while you live
Let your thoughts be with the living.[1]

Notes

CHAPTER ONE   *Matters Personal and Impersonal*

1. Iris Murdoch, *Sartre* (Chatto & Windus, London, 1987), p. 38.
2. Roger Anstey and P. E. H. Hair (ed.), *Liverpool: The African Slave Trade and Abolition*, Occasional Series, Vol. 2 (Historic Society of Lancashire and Cheshire, Liverpool, 1976), p. 65.
3. Ibid., p. 7.
4. Genuine "Dick Sam", *Liverpool and Slavery* (Scouse Press, Liverpool, 1984), p. 28. A centenary reprint of the original edition, published by A. Bowker & Son, Booksellers, 1884.
5. Simone de Beauvoir (trans. Patrick O'Brian), *Adieux: A Farewell to Sartre* (Andre Deutsch/Weidenfeld & Nicolson, London, 1984), p. 445.
6. S. H. Scholl, *150 Jaar Katholieke Arbeidersbeweging in Belgie, 1789–1939* (150 Years of the Catholic Worker Movement in Belgium), Vol. I (Brussels, 1963), p. 120.

CHAPTER TWO   *The Clock of Influence*

1. T. W. Adorno, *Negative Dialectics*. Quoted by Nicholas Lash in *Doing Theology on Dover Beach* (Cambridge University Press, Cambridge, 1978), p. 19.
2. G. Steiner. Quoted by Lash, *Doing Theology on Dover Beach*.
3. Jan Walgrave, *Unfolding Revelation: The Nature of Doctrinal Development* (1972). Quoted by Nicholas Lash in *Change in Focus* (Sheed & Ward, London, 1973), p. 143.
4. P. Claudel, *Positions et Propositions*, Vol. 1 (Gallimard, Paris, 1926), p. 175.

CHAPTER THREE   *A Reflection upon the Christian Roots of Power*

1. Bertrand Russell, *Power* (Allen & Unwin, London, 1938), pp. 25–6.

2. Charles Y. Glock and Rodney Stark, *Religion and Society in Tension* (Chicago, Mass., 1965). Quoted by Joan Brothers in *Religious Institutions* (Longman, Harlow, 1971), p. 1.
3. Mary Douglas, *Risk: Acceptability According to the Social Sciences* (Routledge & Kegan Paul, London, 1986), p. 3.
4. Frederick Coplestone, *Philosophers and Philosophies* (Search Press, Tunbridge Wells, 1976), pp. 73–4.
5. Ibid., p. 74.
6. J. Schmeewin, R. Rorty and Q. Skinner (eds.), *Philosophy in History* (Cambridge University Press, Cambridge, 1984), pp. 6–7.

CHAPTER FOUR   *The Golgotha Experience*

1. For my reflection on religious symbols I rely upon: Paul Tillich (ed. Rollo May), *Symbolism in Religion and Literature* (George Braziller, New York, NY., 1960).
2. *Rules and Constitutions* (Congregation of the Passion, Rome, 1984).
3. Ibid.
4. Fritz Chenderlin, *Do This As My Memorial* (Rome Biblical Institute Press, Rome, 1982), p. 35.
5. I Corinthians 11:26.
6. Dietrich Bonhoeffer. Quoted by G. Guttierez in *Power of the Poor in History* (SCM Press, London, 1983), p. 231.

CHAPTER FIVE   *The God of Golgotha*

1. Leonardo Boff, *Passion of Christ, Passion of the World* (Orbis Books, Maryknoll, NY, 1987), p. 116.

CHAPTER SIX   *The Logic of the System and the Logic of Experience*

1. Dermot Lane, *The Reality of Jesus* (Veritas Publications/Sheed & Ward, London, 1975), p. 41.
2. John 12:20–28.
3. Martin Heidegger (trans. J. Macquarrie and E. Robinson), *Being and Time* (Basil Blackwell, Oxford, 1980), p. 298.

CHAPTER SEVEN   *Pyramids of Power and Powerlessness*

1. Donal Dorr, *Spirituality and Justice* (Gill & McMillan, Dublin, 1984), p. 57.
2. Mark 3, 6.
3. Mark 12, and 14:1–2.
4. Mark 11, 15 and 17–19.
5. E. Gilson, *Unity of Philosophical Experience* (Sheed & Ward, London, 1938), pp. 3ff.
6. T. Kempis, *Imitation of Christ*, Book 1, Chapter 1.
7. Atahulpa Yupanqui. I have been unable to trace the source of this poem, which I read in translation some years ago in a missionary magazine. I offer it here in the form in which I copied it into my own personal notes.
8. Isaiah 1:13.
9. Amos 5:21.
10. Isaiah 58:4.
11. N. Berdyaev, *The Beginning and the End*. Quoted by J. Macquarrie in *Existentialism* (Penguin Books, Harmondsworth, 1972), p. 13.
12. Exodus iii:13–14.
13. G. Vass, *A Theologian in Search of a Philosophy: Understanding Karl Rahner* (Sheed & Ward, London, 1985), pp. 11–13.
14. Charles Péguy (trans. Anne and John Green), *Basic Verities* (Routledge & Kegan Paul, London, 1943), p. 109.
15. G. W. Leibniz, *Confessio Philosophi*.
16. Matthew 7:21.

CHAPTER EIGHT   *Signs of the Times*

1. Y. Congar, *Laypeople in the Church* (Geoffrey Chapman, London, 1959).
2. Roger Aubert, *Christian Centuries*, Vol. 5 (Paulist Press/Darton, Longman & Todd, London, 1978), p. 573.
3. Ibid., p. 572.
4. Aristotle, *The Politics*, Book V (Penguin Classics, Penguin Books, Harmondsworth, 1962), p. 225.
5. Peter Hebblethwaite, *John XXIII, Pope of the Council* (Geoffrey Chapman, London, 1984), p. 485.
6. Walter Abbott, S.J. (ed.), *The Documents of Vatican II* (Geoffrey Chapman, London, 1966).
7. Ibid., p. 704.
8. John XXIII, *Pacem in Terris*, Encyclical letter (Catholic Truth Society, London, 1980), nn. 39–43.

9. Jean Elshtain, *Public Man, Private Woman* (Princeton University Press, Princeton, NJ, 1981), p. 62.

10. Thomas Aquinas, Commentary VIII Book Ethics Aristotle Lect I. This translation taken from Thomas Gilby, *St Thomas Aquinas: Philosophical Texts* (Oxford University Press, Oxford, 1951).

11. *Faith in the City*, Report of the Archbishop of Canterbury's Commission on Urban Priority Areas (Church House Publishing, London, 1985), 12.36.

CHAPTER NINE   *Life's Tensions and Liberation*

1. I am indebted to Dr John McGuckin for his personal notes given to me.

CHAPTER TEN   *The Struggle with Evil*

1. Paul Harrison, *Inside the Inner City* (Penguin Books, Harmondsworth, 1983), pp. 24–5.

CHAPTER ELEVEN   *The Silence of the Inner City*

1. *Policy for the Inner Cities* (HMSO, London, 1977).
2. Michael Mann, *The Sources of Social Power*, Vol. 1 (Cambridge University Press, Cambridge, 1986), p. 6.
3. I Thessalonians 5:19–22.
4. John Paul II, *Solicitudo Rei Socialis*, Encyclical letter (Catholic Truth Society, London, 1987), n. 47.

CHAPTER TWELVE   *Community, Innercityism and the Festive God*

1. *Faith in the City*, Report of the Archbishop of Canterbury's Commission on Urban Priority Areas (Church House Publishing, London, 1985), 4.14.
2. Gertrude Himmelfarb, *The Idea of Poverty* (Faber & Faber, London, 1984), p. 18.
3. Brian McGuiness (ed.), *Wittgenstein and His Times* (Basil Blackwell, Oxford, 1982), p. 113. Quoted by G. H. von Wright in "Wittgenstein in relation to his times" (unpublished essay).

168 JOURNEYING WITH GOD

CHAPTER THIRTEEN *The Festive God*

1. Donald C. P. Senior, *Jesus: A Gospel Portrait* (Pflamn Press, Dayton, OH, 1981), p. 42.
2. Ibid., p. 47 (Mark 2:13–17).
3. Matthew 20:25ff.
4. Personal communication from Dr John McGuckin.
5. Ibid.

CHAPTER FOURTEEN *Conversation*

1. I Corinthians 11:23–5.
2. Mark 15:1.
3. M. Blondel (trans. Oliva Blanchette), *Action: Essay on a Critique of Life and Science of Practice* (1893), (University of Notre Dame Press, Notre Dame, Ind., 1984).
4. *Theology Digest*, Vol. 32, No. 3, pp. 203–17.
5. Ibid., p. 206.
6. Ibid., p. 214.
7. T. McCarthy, *The Critical Theory of Jurgen Habermas* (Polity Press, Oxford, 1978).

CHAPTER FIFTEEN *An Ecumenism Beyond Ecumenism*

1. The author of this prayer is anonymous.